Stack, Shuffle, and Slide

A New Technique for Stack the Deck Quilts

Karla Alexander

Martingale®
Create with Confidence

Acknowledgments

My husband, Don, has helped every step of the way, throughout books, studio projects, and crazy schedules. He is more important to me than all my quilts stacked up together into one big pile—and that would be one tall pile! Thank you, Don!

I'm also grateful for my friends: Loretta, the quilting wizard; Sally, who often helps with piecing and borders at the tail end of a book; and Leslie, who is always willing to collect my leftover trial-and-error blocks and work them into quilts for her own use as well as for the Mid Valley Quilt Guild of Salem. Thanks to each of you!

Thanks to my technical editor, Ellen Pahl, for her excellent guidance, and to the staff at Martingale for their combined efforts to help me create *Stack, Shuffle, and Slide*.

I would like to thank Jean Wells for her excellent advice when she encouraged me to pause while creating my work, to slow down long enough to determine and study the next step. This let me see if each project needed additional color, a different design element, or if it was finished. The message is invaluable. Thank you, Jean!

Stack, Shuffle, and Slide: A New Technique for Stack the Deck Quilts
© 2014 by Karla Alexander

Martingale®
19021 120th Ave. NE, Ste. 102
Bothell, WA 98011-9511 USA
ShopMartingale.com

Mission Statement

Dedicated to providing quality products and service to inspire creativity.

Credits

PRESIDENT AND CEO: Tom Wierzbicki

EDITOR IN CHIEF: Mary V. Green

DESIGN DIRECTOR: Paula Schlosser

MANAGING EDITOR: Karen Costello Soltys

ACQUISITIONS EDITOR: Karen M. Burns

TECHNICAL EDITOR: Ellen Pahl

COPY EDITOR: Melissa Bryan

PRODUCTION MANAGER: Regina Girard

COVER AND INTERIOR DESIGNER: Connor Chin

PHOTOGRAPHER: Brent Kane

ILLUSTRATOR: Lisa Lauch

Printed in China
19 18 17 16 15 14   8 7 6 5 4 3 2 1

Library of Congress Cataloging-in-Publication Data is available upon request.

ISBN: 978-1-60468-235-9

CONTENTS

INTRODUCTION

I had a lot of fun making the quilts for this book. Well, I always have a lot of fun making my quilts, but this time I took a slightly different approach to color placement. In my previous books, I sometimes used a method I call the controlled shuffle, but for most of the designs, my stack-shuffle-slice technique afforded only minimal control over the different values and colors in each block. With this book I'm introducing a new concept I call "Slip 'n' Slide," which is explained on page 6. I still make blocks with a wide variety of strip widths and colors, but with my new method, I have full control over color and value placement. This opens the door to a bunch of new designs. If I want a block to read light to dark, or I want to isolate dark in only one spot, I now have that option.

Another difference you'll find in this book is that I don't do as much chain piecing as I've done in the past. Instead, many of the blocks are made one at a time. This gives you the opportunity to reshuffle each layer as you go in case you want to move the colors around.

One thing hasn't changed, though: I encourage you, as always, to find your own path and create your own journey. May your quilting energy be renewed and refreshed with each new project you choose to take on. Enjoy!

STACK THE DECK

All the projects in this book use my stack the deck technique. You stack fabric squares or rectangles, all right side up, into a fabric "deck" and then slice the deck into various shapes. The shapes are then shuffled and each layer is sewn back together. This method gives you the advantage of using many different fabrics without having to mess around with a lot of math or odd-shaped templates. If you want to make more blocks than the pattern calls for, you can usually start with the same number of squares or rectangles as you would like completed blocks. This makes it fun to check out your stash and rediscover a few favorite pieces of which you have only a small amount left. As long as you can cut the fabric into a square or rectangle as required in the quilt pattern, you can usually use it. What a great option!

Stacking the Decks

Once you've cut the required number of squares or rectangles, stack the pieces right side up for rotary cutting as indicated in the project instructions. Stack the colors as directed for each individual quilt. Before cutting, I like to lay out my deck, fanning the layers on top of one another to make sure I have the correct number of fabrics and colors in the deck and that I like the mix. Once you're satisfied with your choices, stack the fabrics neatly, lining up the edges as perfectly as you can. Place a straight pin through all layers in each deck to keep them together.

Slicing the Decks

Each project gives specific instructions for cutting, shuffling, and sewing. Slice the decks apart first, following the order given. In some projects, you will make a few extra blocks in order to keep an equal balance of fabric in a deck. The extra blocks give you more choices in the final quilt layout.

Slice and sew one deck at a time. This gives you the opportunity to make changes for variety along the way. I usually like to vary my cutting with each deck. Use a chalk marker to draw the cutting lines on your decks unless the instructions call for an exact width or length. You can brush away the lines if you don't like them and redraw until you're satisfied.

If you are unable to cut through the multiple layers of fabric, stack your deck, and then remove two layers and cut them as directed. Carefully use the cut pieces as templates, placing them on top of another two layers and continuing to cut in the same manner. If the deck is long and narrow, I often cut just a few layers at a time.

Shuffling the Decks

Shuffling refers to rearranging the fabric segments once they've been cut. By shuffling each stack of fabrics in a specific order, you will create a variation of fabrics in each layer to make up a block. Each project provides specific instructions on which and how many pieces to shuffle. The number on each piece indicates how many pieces or layers from the top of the stack you move to the bottom of the stack. An *L* means to leave that stack as it is.

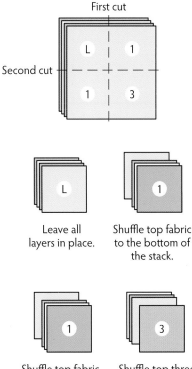

//Slip 'n' Slide

In addition to the initial shuffle, many of the designs in this book also use a second shuffle that I call "Slip 'n' Slide." This technique enables you to have more control over the color arrangements in the blocks. The instructions for each quilt will guide you through the specific stacking, cutting, and shuffling process. Rather than chain sewing, however, generally you'll sew one layer at a time into a block. When you sew each layer, you will always keep the color order the same (unless directed otherwise), but the strips of each color will be a different width from layer to layer. It's easy and it's like magic!

As an example, let's say that you have a deck of five squares:

1. Stack, slice, and shuffle the deck as directed.

Stack the deck.   Make 4 cuts.

Shuffle.

2. Draw a line with a chalk marker across the top shuffled layer (layer 1) before you pick up the pieces. This will ensure that you haven't accidentally dipped into the next layer. Place the top layer of pieces next to your sewing machine and sew them together.

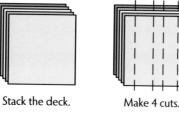

Mark and sew layer 1.

3. Pick up the pieces in layer 2 and place them next to your machine. Slide the piece on the right side of the deck to the left side to maintain the color order, and sew the pieces together. In layer 3, slide the *two* pieces from the right side to the left, and sew the pieces together. Continue in this manner until all the layers have been sewn together into blocks.

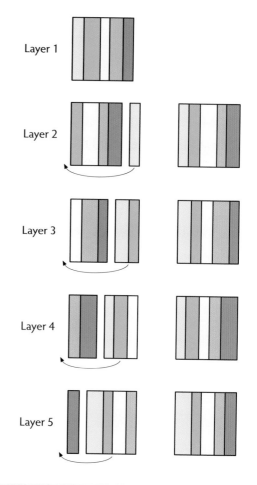

Layer 1

Layer 2

Layer 3

Layer 4

Layer 5

Mixed-Up Strips

If your layers get mixed up, or you become confused, lay out your strips side by side and measure them. The total width of all the strips in one layer, before being sewn, should always equal the beginning width of the square or rectangle.

Preparing a Paper Layout

After shuffling, it's helpful to make a paper layout. Place the stacks in order and pin each one to a piece of paper through all layers. Be sure to keep the segments in the exact order and position in which you shuffled them. Once the segments are secure, use a pencil and trace along the cutting lines onto the paper. The pins will help keep the segments in order and the lines will create a template for reference. For pieces that are too long or too big to pin to a regular piece of paper, simply tape two or more pieces of paper together. If you are working with long strips, you can just pin the top edges of the stack to paper, penciling each strip width on the paper for reference.

When using the Slip 'n' Slide method and piecing one layer at a time, it's essential that you note the color order of the strips as well as the width to avoid mix-ups. The color order will remain the same, which means you'll be using the Slip 'n' Slide method on each layer as you sew. You can always add up the strip widths as noted in "Mixed-Up Strips" on page 6 if something gets out of order.

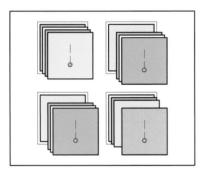

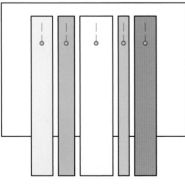

Strip widths: 2", 1½", 3", 1", 2"
Color order: turquoise, green,
cream, medium blue, teal

Sewing the Blocks

Sew the blocks as directed with each project. Sometimes the sewing order is the exact opposite of the order in which the segments were cut, but not always, so follow the instructions closely. It's important to keep the segment stacks in their shuffled order while sewing; otherwise you'll end up duplicating a fabric or strip width unintentionally. I strongly recommend that you place a safety pin in the top layer of the first segment to be sewn. This way, if you are chain piecing you'll always know which pieces belong to the top layer, and you'll know that the sewn segments are in the correct sequence. The projects are written with instructions to chain piece, or sew layer by layer. Both are suggestions, and I encourage you to do whatever works best for you.

Chain Piecing

Use chain piecing as indicated in the project instructions. Chain piece by flipping piece 2 right sides together with piece 1, and then sewing along the edge. Without breaking the thread, sew pieces 1 and 2 from the next layer together. Continue with each layer, sewing piece 1 to piece 2 without cutting the thread in between.

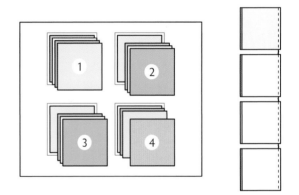

In some blocks, you will need to sew pieces together to create a unit and then join the units. Using a Four Patch block as an example, sew the top pieces together first to create a unit. Return the unit to the paper layout and pin, leaving the safety pin in place to identify the top layer. Sew the pieces to complete the lower units and then chain piece the units together.

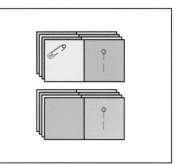

Flippers for Flat Seams

When you want to sew two units together and the seam allowances of both units are pressed in the same direction, create a "flipper." To do this, flip one of the seam allowances in the opposite direction and clip up to, but not through, the stitching line. Press the clipped portion flat and then sew the seam. Seam allowances nest better and lie flatter when the seam allowances are pressed in opposing directions.

//Trimming the Blocks

In most of the projects, the blocks or block units will need to be trimmed before they are sewn together. This is due to seam allowances; the pieced segments shrink up and are smaller when added to unpieced segments or segments with fewer seams. Trim the excess fabric as instructed to create even edges. If size is not critical, trim all of the blocks to the size of your smallest block.

Place a ruler on top of the block and trim two sides. Rotate the block 180°, align the trimmed edges with the correct measurement on the ruler, and trim the remaining two sides.

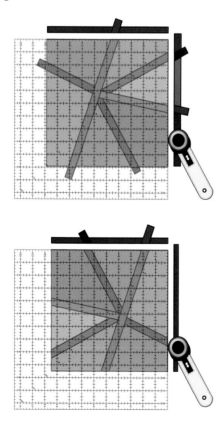

If the blocks are larger than your ruler, use the measurements on your cutting mat.

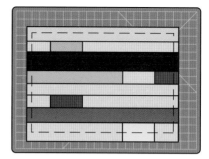

WWGD (What Would Grandma Do?)

Well, we know for sure that Grandma wouldn't have had a big stash or yards of 42"-wide fabric to choose from. Most likely, she would have worked with flour and feed sacks along with a few worn shirts or other old clothing items—anything she could muster up to make into a quilt. She would have improvised and mixed things up, and her quilts would rarely have been made from a coordinated collection of fabrics.

I love the idea of spontaneously adding a favorite piece of fabric to a block. I think it makes a quilt more interesting. Maybe I have just one or two squares left of a favorite fabric; I like the option of being able to use that fabric if it fits with my project. I never hesitate to improvise. That's why in many of the projects in this book, you might detect more prints than are listed in the fabric requirements. I encourage you to give this approach a try. Look at each block individually and think, WWGD? Then make each one the way you like.

ASSEMBLY AND FINISHING

Once all your blocks are complete, it's time for the quilt layout. Arrange your blocks in rows according to the project instructions, or choose your own arrangement. Enjoy a completely new creation by putting your own spin on it. If you want to orient the blocks in the opposite way or position them in a different pattern, do it!

Once you're pleased with the arrangement, join your blocks into rows, matching the seams within the blocks as needed. I like to pin as I go to prevent any surprises once I'm done. Press the seam allowances in the opposite direction from row to row so that opposing seams butt against each other. Join the rows of blocks together into pairs, and then sew the pairs together. Begin your sewing at opposite ends from row to row to prevent warping that can occur when you always begin sewing from the same end.

//Adding Borders

Some of the quilts in this book have pieced borders and some have traditional borders. In my opinion, borders are always optional, not a necessity. You can leave them off if you choose, or add more of them, or make them wider or narrower. Always keep the overall design of your quilt in mind and give careful thought to when or when not to add a border according to what you like. Borders should make a quilt better and more beautiful, not just bigger! If you feel like your quilt is perfect without borders, skip them! On the other hand, if you find an awesome print that will make your quilt look that much more fabulous, then go for it and add a border.

//Making the Design Your Own

Most of the projects in this book allow for variations to the original design. I encourage you to create your own work, and hopefully the designs in this book will help you on your way. Try to allow your quilt to evolve as you go. Change it up if you like by adding different colors, more blocks, or a border. Arrange the blocks in a different setting. Take into account the size of your quilt and what you would like to use it for, make changes along the way, and enjoy.

I like to compare the quilts in this book to making soup. Keep adding to the mix until you are pleased. Whether you add borders, more colors, more blocks, or a screaming off-the-wall color for a binding, make it your own and work it until you are happy!

//Quilting and Binding

There are many good sources of information about finishing your quilt. In order to provide as many quilt projects in this book as possible, the details of basting, quilting, and binding are not included. For guidance with these steps or any aspect of basic quiltmaking, visit ShopMartingale.com/HowtoQuilt for free, downloadable information.

It's a WRAP

At the end of every project, I always seem to experience a moment of judgment and reflection. I like to call it the WRAP, and I encourage you to make it part of your own quiltmaking experience:

Wonder . . . about what the quilt might have been like with a different fabric, pattern, or shade here or there. Also, think about what the quilt's future will be. Where will it go and to how many people will it bring joy?

Reflect . . . on what you did best, as well as what you learned. What will you do better next time? Do you still wish you had fixed that one mistake, or are you glad you left it alone?

Appreciate . . . what you've done. You're participating in a unique and wonderful craft that is an important part of our culture.

Plan . . . the next step in your quilting journey. Are you going to jump into another project right away? Or is it time to relax, enjoy your accomplishment, and dream about what you might do next?

And here's one final piece of advice as you congratulate yourself for your freshly completed quilt: if you possibly can, wrap yourself up in it!

WREN RAILS

There are two key things to know about the blocks in this Rail Fence quilt. First, the darkest prints will always be on the outside edges of the block and the lightest will always be in the center. Second, each block in one deck is different from one to the next. The width of the rails always changes—but the order of the assorted fabrics will always stay the same. The blocks are also easy to manipulate. If there is a color you want to switch out in a block, you can replace it with another strip of the same size and value from your scraps. I chose colors that reminded me of newly hatched birds with their feathers poking out of their pink bellies. This is a great quilt if you need a quick project with outstanding results!

Finished quilt: 54½" x 72½"
Finished block: 9" x 9"

//Materials

Yardage is based on 42"-wide fabric. Fat quarters measure approximately 18" x 22".

1 fat quarter *each* of 4 different dark-value prints: black, brown, or blue

1 fat quarter *each* of 4 different medium-value prints: brown, gray, or blue

1 fat quarter *each* of 4 different medium-light-value prints: pink, beige, or gray

⅓ yard *each* of 2 different dark-value prints: black, brown, or blue

⅓ yard *each* of 2 different medium-value prints: brown, gray, or blue

⅓ yard *each* of 2 different medium-light-value prints: pink, beige, or gray

⅓ yard of light-value print: creamy white or light gray

1 fat quarter *each* of 2 different light-value prints: creamy white or light gray

⅝ yard of fabric for binding

4¾ yards of fabric for backing

63" x 81" piece of batting

Fabric Tips

To make this quilt really shine, choose an assortment of small- to medium-scale prints ranging from dark to light and back to dark again. I chose a gradation of cool colors from black and brown to gray and blue for the medium and dark edges of the blocks, and I placed light, creamy beiges and pinks in the block centers. To help make your choices, layer your fabrics vertically, and then stand back and take a look. Take a quick picture with a digital camera or cell phone for a different view. The run of colors needs to gradate from dark to light and dark again. Fold your selections into 3" to 4" widths and then arrange them in the exact order they will appear in your blocks. This is a great stash quilt if you have one. Simply begin with the exact number and value of rectangles specified in the cutting list. Each rectangle is equivalent to one completed block. If you want more blocks, you'll need to cut another deck, always working with seven layers.

"Wren Rails," designed and pieced by Karla Alexander, machine quilted by Loretta Orsborn

//Cutting

From *each* of the 7 print ⅓-yard pieces, cut:

1 strip, 10" x 42"; crosscut into 3 rectangles,
10" x 13" (21 total)*

From *each* of the 14 print fat quarters, cut:

2 rectangles, 10" x 13" (28 total)*

From the binding fabric, cut:

7 strips, 2½" x 42"

If you are working from your stash, cut a total of 49 rectangles, 10" x 13", as follows: 7 light, 14 medium-light, 14 medium, and 14 dark.

//Making the Blocks

1. Arrange the 10" x 13" rectangles right side up into seven decks of seven layers each. Each deck should contain seven different fabrics with no duplications. Stack the layers in this order within each deck: dark, medium, medium-light, light, medium-light, medium, and dark. Each fabric assortment can be different from deck to deck, but keep the values in the same order.

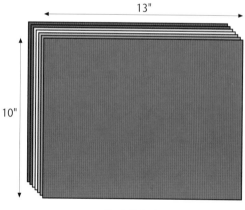

Stack 7 decks.

2. Work with one stack at a time, lining up the edges as evenly as possible. Make six cuts through all seven layers as shown, keeping each stack at least 1¼" wide.

Make 6 cuts.

3. Beginning at the left end of the deck, leave the first stack in place (L). Peel the top layer from the second stack and place it at the bottom of the stack. Peel the top two layers from the third stack and place them at the bottom of that stack. Continue in this manner, shuffling an additional layer each time. You should end up with seven different prints showing on the top layer, in values ranging from dark to light and back to dark. Make a paper layout as described on page 7 and pin the layers to the paper.

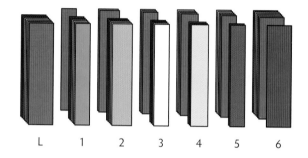

L   1   2   3   4   5   6

Make a Note

It's a good idea to write down the widths of the seven stacks. That way, if you happen to get mixed up, you can always measure your pieces to get back on track. The sum of the widths will always be 13" (the width of the original rectangles). You can also mark a horizontal line across each layer of the deck with a chalk marker before sewing to identify the layer you are working with.

4. Peel the top layer from each of the stacks and sew the pieces together in order. Press the seam allowances to one side. Don't worry if the edges don't match up perfectly—you will trim them to size later. Set the block aside.

5. Move the entire right-hand stack to the left end of the deck as shown to maintain the value order. You should always begin and end with a dark value and have the lightest stack in the center.

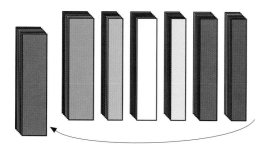

6. Continue sewing one layer at a time, repositioning the right-hand stack to the left end of the deck after you complete each layer. The value order will not change; only the size of the pieces will be different. Press the seam allowances to one side.

7. Repeat with all seven decks to make 49 blocks.

8. Use a square ruler to trim each block to 9½" x 9½". Don't worry if your blocks don't turn out to be exactly 9½"; just be consistent and trim them all to the same size.

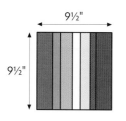

//Assembling the Quilt Top

1. Refer to the quilt assembly diagram, right, for block placement. Arrange the blocks into eight horizontal rows of six blocks each, alternating the blocks with vertical and horizontal seams. Rearrange the blocks until you are satisfied. You will have one extra block.

2. Pin and sew the blocks together into rows. Press the seam allowances toward the blocks with the horizontal seams. Pin and sew the rows together

in sets of two each, then in two sections of four, and then join the sections. Press the seam allowances in one direction.

Quilt assembly

//Finishing the Quilt

Layer and baste your quilt top with backing and batting, and then add quilting and binding.

For details on any of these steps, go to ShopMartingale.com/HowtoQuilt for free downloadable information.

SIMPLE SIMON

As the name suggests, the construction of this quilt is very simple. Rails of unequal sizes step down across the quilt top, creating a design with geometric charm. You could easily make this quilt larger or smaller by simply increasing or decreasing the size of the squares used for the stacked fabric decks. Cutting and sewing additional fabric decks for a bigger quilt is also an option.

Finished quilt: 59" x 74"
Finished block: 7½" x 7½"

//Materials

Yardage is based on 42"-wide fabric.

⅓ yard *each* of 4 different medium- to dark-gray solids for blocks*

⅓ yard *each* of 4 different medium-green solids (lime to avocado) for blocks*

⅓ yard *each* of 4 different off-white solids for blocks*

⅛ yard *each* of dark-blue, turquoise, purple, and black solids for block accent strips

1 yard of dark-gray solid for outer border

⅞ yard of black solid for middle border and binding

⅝ yard of light-gray solid for inner border

4¾ yards of fabric for backing

67" x 82" piece of batting

One fat quarter of each fabric will also work.

Fabric Tips

I previewed fabric for this quilt by pinning fabrics side by side on my design wall and then standing back approximately 10 feet to decide what I liked. It's important to have good contrast from color group to color group. Small- to medium-scale prints as well as solids work well with this design. While the materials list calls for four gray, four green, and four off-white fabrics, you could choose a different set of colors and use as many different prints as you like. Just make sure you can organize your selections into three distinctly different and contrasting color groups.

//Cutting

From *each* of the 12 solids for blocks, cut:
   1 strip, 8" x 42"; crosscut into 4 squares, 8" x 8" (48 total)

From *each* of the 4 solids for accent strips, cut:
   3 strips, 1" x 42"; crosscut into 12 strips, 1" x 8" (48 total)

From the light-gray solid, cut:
   6 strips, 2¾" x 42"

From the black solid, cut:
   6 strips, 1" x 42"
   7 strips, 2½" x 42"

From the dark-gray solid, cut:
   6 strips, 4½" x 42"

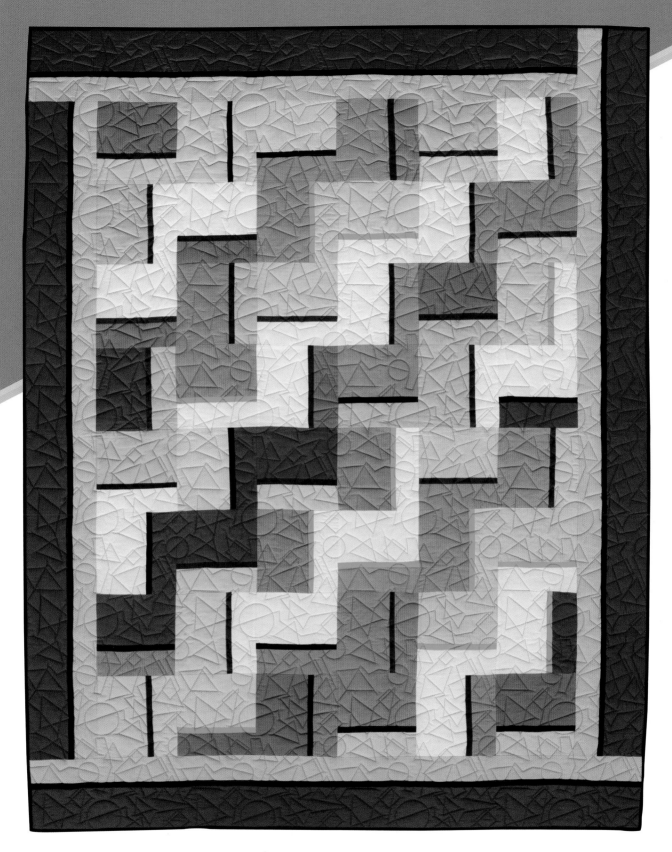

"Simple Simon," designed and pieced by Karla Alexander, machine quilted by Loretta Orsborn

//Making the Blocks

1. Randomly choose an off-white, a green, and a dark-gray 8" square. Layer the squares right side up into a deck with the white on the bottom, the green in the middle, and the dark gray on top. Make a total of 16 fabric decks with three layers in each.

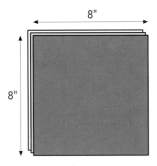

Stack 16 decks.

2. Measure and cut a 2¾" x 8" strip from the left edge of a deck, cutting through all three layers.

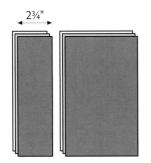

Make 1 cut.

3. Remove the dark-gray 2¾" x 8" strip from the top and place it at the bottom of the stack. This will result in three layers as shown.

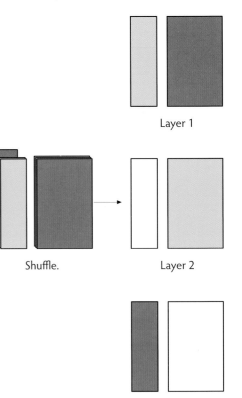

Layer 1

Shuffle.   Layer 2

Layer 3

4. Randomly choose three different 1" x 8" accent strips. Keeping the decks from step 3 in their shuffled order, chain piece an accent strip to the right edge of each 2¾" x 8" strip.

5. Keeping the stacks in their original shuffled order, add the larger piece to the right edge of each accent strip. Press the seam allowances toward the accent strip.

6. Repeat steps 2–5 with the remaining decks to make a total of 48 blocks.

7. Separate the blocks into three piles as shown, with 16 each of blocks A, B, and C. The A blocks will have a narrow green strip with a wide gray strip, the B blocks will have a narrow gray strip with a wide white strip, and the C blocks will have a narrow white strip with a wide green strip.

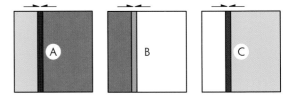

//Assembling the Quilt Top

1. Referring to the quilt layout, arrange the blocks into eight horizontal rows of six blocks each. The widest strip in each block should be positioned at the top or the left.

2. Pin and sew the blocks into rows. Press the seam allowances in opposite directions from row to row. Pin and sew the rows together in sets of two each, then into two sections of four, and then join the sections. Press the seam allowances to one side.

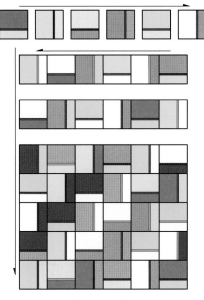

Quilt assembly

//Adding the Borders

1. Remove the selvage ends from all of the light-gray, black, and dark-gray border strips. Sew the strips together end to end to make one long strip of each color. Press the seam allowances open.

2. Sew the strips together side by side to make one long strip, positioning the black strip in the middle. Offset each strip by about 3" to prevent seam allowances from lining up next to each other. Press the seam allowances toward the black middle-border strip.

3. Measure the length of the quilt top through the center and cut one border strip to that measurement. Sew it to the left side of the quilt. Press the seam allowances toward the border. Measure the width of the quilt top through the center, including the border strip just added, and cut one border strip to that measurement. Sew it to the top of the quilt. Continue to measure, cut, and add the two remaining border strips, working in a clockwise manner. Press the seam allowances toward the borders.

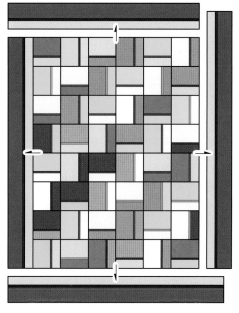

Adding borders

//Finishing the Quilt

Layer and baste your quilt top with backing and batting, and then add quilting and binding.

For details on any of these steps, go to ShopMartingale.com/HowtoQuilt for free downloadable information.

ROAD TO NOWHERE

The entire time I worked on this quilt, my mind was filled with images of the various things the design reminded me of—street maps, bridges, pick-up sticks, you name it. What makes it fun is that you can decide just how "congested" you want each block to be. It doesn't matter how many accent lines you add; the overall block size will not change. I chose to make a diagonal path through my quilt that somewhat resembles a map, with the congestion centered in the middle and thinning out as it continues into the corners. You can incorporate a lot of accent lines or just a few, deciding as you go. You can even add additional lines once your blocks are laid out. I added several more in the blocks and even in the border to continue the traffic pattern diagonally.

Finished quilt: 55" x 70½"
Finished block: 15½" x 15½"

//Materials

Yardage is based on 42"-wide fabric. Fat quarters measure approximately 18" x 22".

⅓ yard *each* of 6 different light solids for block A

1 fat quarter *each* of 6 different light solids for block B

¼ yard *each* of 9 different prints and stripes for block accent strips

⅞ yard of gray solid for border

⅝ yard of fabric for binding

3¾ yards of fabric for backing

63" x 79" piece of batting

Fabric Tips

For the background, I chose a mix of six different light solids that blended well. For the accent lines, I chose three different blues and two different reds that appeared mostly solid from a distance. I included four more prints that were mostly white with a bit of accent color in each. If you have a fabric stash, this would be a good time to use it. I think this design would be equally awesome if the colors were switched, with pathways of light prints traveling across a contrasting black and dark-blue background.

//Cutting

From *each* of the 6 solid ⅓-yard pieces, cut:
  1 strip, 9½" x 42"; crosscut into:
    4 rectangles, 8" x 9½" (24 total)
    1 square, 5½" x 5½" (6 total)
    1 square, 2" x 2" (6 total)

From *each* of the 6 solid fat quarters, cut:
  1 square, 17" x 17" (6 total)

From *each* of the 9 prints and stripes, cut:
  4 strips, 1" x 42" (36 total)

From the gray solid, cut:
  6 strips, 4½" x 42"

From the binding fabric, cut:
  7 strips, 2½" x 42"

"Road to Nowhere," designed and pieced by Karla Alexander, machine quilted by Loretta Orsborn

Making the A Blocks

Each A block is made up of four pieced rectangular blocks and a center square. These blocks create the diagonal path (the area of most "congestion") through the center of the quilt.

1. Arrange and neatly stack six different solid 8" x 9½" rectangles right side up into a fabric deck. Repeat to make a total of four decks. Use a different arrangement of colors in each deck.

2. Refer to the illustrations for cutting suggestions. You can follow my cuts exactly by referring to the photograph or make more or fewer cuts. Keep all your cuts at least 1" from the outer edge and at least 1" apart. Other than that, the placement of each is your choice. Premark your lines with a chalk marker. You can lay the 1"-wide accent strips over the top of your rectangle to get a rough idea of how it will look once you cut and sew it back together.

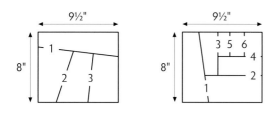

3. Shuffle the deck by removing the top layer from one section and placing it at the bottom of the stack. Continue shuffling in whatever order you like; it's OK to duplicate of one or two fabrics, as they will be separated by an accent strip. I often created a combination that made an L shape. You can control the color in each block, as you like.

4. Choose a 1" accent strip for the first seam to be sewn. You will sew the pieces back together in reverse order of cutting. Lay the strip over the top of the cut and trim 1" longer than the cut. Cut six, one for each layer of the stack. You can use the same fabric, or a different one for each layer.

5. Place a safety pin in the upper corner of the first piece to identify the top layer of your deck. You may also want to number the pieces with a chalk marker to keep them organized.

6. Using an accurate ¼" seam allowance, chain sew the 1" strips right sides together to the first piece in each layer of the deck. Remove from the sewing

machine and pull all six sections toward you (without cutting the thread between the blocks).

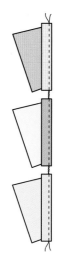

7. Open up the accent strips and add the next piece for all six layers. Remove from the sewing machine and cut the threads between the blocks, keeping them in their shuffled order. Press the seam allowances toward the accent strips. Trim the ends of the accent strips even with the edges of the pieces as needed.

8. Continue to add the accent strips between the pieces until the blocks are complete. Sometimes you will need to piece the blocks in sections, and then sew the sections together in the end.

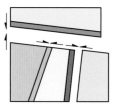

9. Make a total of 24 blocks and trim each one to 7½" x 9".

10. Arrange four of the blocks from step 9 around a 2" square as shown on page 21 to create the larger block. Beginning with the lower-right block, sew the block to the center square using a partial seam. Finger-press the seam allowances toward the small square. Add the second block as shown. Finger-press the seam allowances toward the center square. Work in a clockwise direction to add the third and fourth blocks. Place the edges of the

fourth and first blocks right sides together. Begin sewing at the partial seam and continue to the outer edge to complete the partial seam. Press the seam allowances toward the center square.

11. Repeat step 10 to make a total of three blocks.

12. Repeat step 10 to make three additional blocks, but sew these blocks in the reverse order, counter-clockwise, as shown.

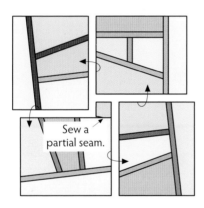

//Making the B Blocks

1. Arrange and neatly stack six different solid 17" squares right side up into a fabric deck.

2. Refer to the illustration for cutting suggestions. You can follow my cuts exactly or make more or fewer cuts. Keep all your cuts at least 1" from the outer edge and at least 1" apart. Premark your lines with a chalk marker. You can lay the accent strips over the top of your rectangle to get a rough idea of how the block will look once you cut and sew it back together.

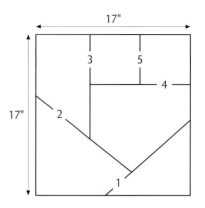

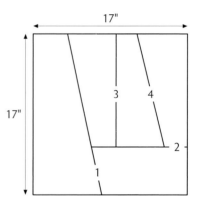

3. Referring to page 20, repeat steps 3–8 of "Making the A Blocks." Trim the blocks to 16" x 16".

//Making the Mini Border Blocks

1. Arrange and neatly stack the six light 5½" squares right side up into a fabric deck.

2. Refer to the illustration for guidance on where to make your cuts. You can follow my cuts exactly or make more or fewer cuts. Keep all your cuts a minimum of 1" from the outer edge and at least 1" apart. Premark your lines with a chalk marker if desired.

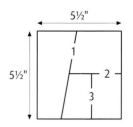

3. Referring to page 20, repeat steps 3–8 of "Making the A Blocks." Trim the blocks to 4½" x 4½".

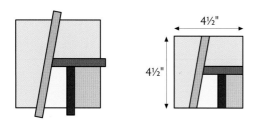

//Assembling the Quilt Top

1. Referring to the quilt assembly diagram, right, for block placement, arrange the blocks into four horizontal rows. Once the blocks are in the layout, you can cut and add additional accent strips if you feel the design needs a bit more congestion in some areas.

2. Pin and sew the blocks into rows. Press the seam allowances in opposite directions from row to row. Pin and sew the rows together in two sets of two, and then join the sections. Press the seam allowances in one direction.

//Adding the Borders

1. Sew the gray 4½" x 42" strips together end to end to make one long strip. Press the seam allowances to one side.

2. Audition the border strip next to the quilt center. Cut the border strip across the width and add 1" accent strips randomly, wherever you think a bit more congestion might add visually to the overall design.

3. Pin and sew a mini block to one end of the border strip. Then measure the length of the quilt top and cut one strip to that measurement, including the mini block. Pin and sew the border to one long side of the quilt top. Repeat for the other side, adding the mini block to the opposite end. Press the seam allowances toward the border.

4. Sew two mini blocks together and add to one end of the remaining border strip. Then measure the width of the quilt top, including the side borders, and cut one strip to that measurement, including the two mini blocks. Pin and sew the border to the top edge of the quilt top. Repeat for the bottom edge. Press the seam allowances toward the border.

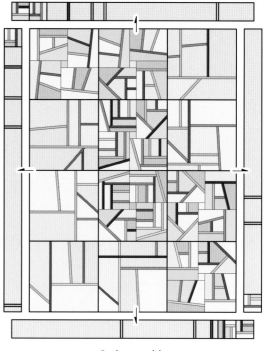

Quilt assembly

//Finishing the Quilt

Layer and baste your quilt top with backing and batting, and then add quilting and binding.

For details on any of these steps, go to ShopMartingale.com/HowtoQuilt for free downloadable information.

GOLD RUSH

This simple quilt design lets the fabrics do all the work. Once you have chosen your preferred colors and the cutting process is out of the way, you'll be surprised how quickly it comes together. It's entirely possible to cut and piece this quilt in one afternoon!

Finished quilt: 67½" x 85½"
Finished block: 9" x 9"

//Materials

Yardage is based on 42"-wide fabric. Fat quarters measure approximately 18" x 22".

⅝ yard *each* of 2 different black medium-scale prints for blocks

⅝ yard *each* of 2 different gold medium-scale prints for blocks

1 fat quarter *each* of 4 different red or dark-pink medium- to small-scale prints for blocks*

⅜ yard *each* of 2 different black medium-scale prints for blocks

⅜ yard *each* of 2 different gold medium-scale prints for blocks

1⅜ yards of dark multicolored print for outer border

½ yard of dark-charcoal tone-on-tone print for inner border

⅔ yard of fabric for binding

5¼ yards of fabric for backing

76" x 94" piece of batting

You can use ⅝ yard of a single print if variety isn't a priority.

Fabric Tips

Choose two main colors for your quilt. I chose black and gold to create a strong contrast. You will need a mix of six different prints for each color. Select medium-scale prints that feature uneven designs and multiple colors. The six prints in each group should blend together somewhat, but not so well that they appear to be the same fabric. When you are cutting, you can decide which prints you want to showcase the most and use those for the larger pieces. The rectangles and squares that cascade diagonally across the quilt top are small-scale or tone-on-tone prints, which serve to separate the two primary colors.

//Cutting

From *each* of the 2 black ⅝-yard pieces, cut:
1 strip, 11" x 42"; crosscut into 1 rectangle, 11" x 20" (2 total). From the remaining piece, cut 2 strips, 5½" x 20"; crosscut into 4 rectangles, 5½" x 9½" (8 total).
1 strip, 5½" x 42"; crosscut into 4 rectangles, 5½" x 9½" (8 total)

Continued on page 25

"Gold Rush," designed and pieced by Karla Alexander, machine quilted by Loretta Orsborn

Continued from page 23

From *each* of the 2 black ⅜-yard pieces, cut:
1 strip, 11" x 42"; cut 1 rectangle, 11" x 20" (2 total)
From the remaining piece, cut 2 strips, 5½" x 20";
 crosscut into 4 rectangles, 5½" x 9½" (8 total)

From *each* of the 2 gold ⅝-yard pieces, cut:
1 strip, 5½" x 42"; crosscut into 4 rectangles,
 5½" x 9½" (8 total)
1 strip, 11" x 42"; cut 1 rectangle, 11" x 20" (2 total)
From the remaining piece, cut 2 strips, 5½" x 20";
 crosscut into 4 rectangles, 5½" x 9½" (8 total)

From *each* of the 2 gold ⅜-yard pieces, cut:
1 strip, 11" x 42"; cut 1 rectangle, 11" x 20" (2 total)
From the remaining piece, cut 2 strips, 5½" x 20";
 crosscut into 4 rectangles, 5½" x 9½" (8 total)

From *each* of the 4 red or pink fat quarters, cut:
1 rectangle, 11" x 20" (4 total)

From the dark-charcoal print, cut:
7 strips, 2" x 42"

From the dark multicolored print, cut:
8 strips, 5½" x 42"

From the binding fabric, cut:
8 strips, 2½" x 42"

//Making the Blocks

1. Arrange the 11" x 20" rectangles right side up into two decks of six layers each. Each deck should contain six different fabrics and be stacked as follows: red or dark pink on the bottom, black, gold, red or dark pink, black, and gold on top. Line up the edges as perfectly as you can.

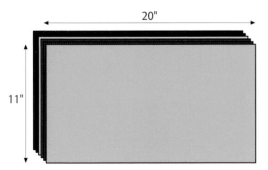

Stack 2 decks.

2. Cut each deck twice to create three 20"-long strips. I cut the first deck using these measurements: 3¾", 4", and 3¼". For the second deck I used these measurements: 3¼", 4¼", and 3½". You can use different measurements if you like; just make sure that each strip is at least 2" wide.

3. Shuffle one deck by peeling the top layer from the upper stack and placing it at the bottom of that stack. Peel the top two layers from the center stack and place them at the bottom of that stack. Leave the third stack (gold) as it is.

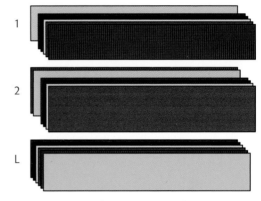

Make 2 cuts and shuffle.

4. Each layer will consist of a gold, a dark pink or red, and a black strip. Working with one layer at a time, remove and sew the top three strips together, positioning the red or dark pink between a black print and a gold print. Always sew the strips together in that order, keeping the dark pink or red strip in the center. When you get to the second layer, slip and slide the red or dark pink so that it is between the gold and the black. Continue sewing until all layers have been sewn together into strip sets. Press the seam allowances toward the darkest print. Trim the height of the strip sets to 9½".

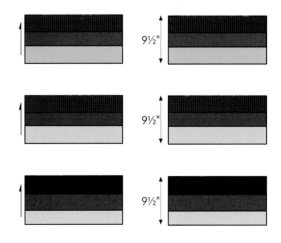

5. Crosscut each strip set into four 4½"-wide segments. Repeat the shuffling, sewing, and cutting process with the remaining deck. You'll have a total of 48 segments.

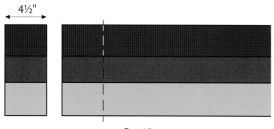

Cut 48.

6. Pin and sew black 5½" x 9½" rectangles to the right side of 12 segments from step 5 with black at the top to make block A. Pin and sew black print rectangles to the right side of 12 segments with gold at the top to make block B. Repeat to sew gold rectangles to the right side of 12 segments with black at the top to make block C. Sew gold rectangles to the right side of 12 segments with gold at the top to make block D. Press the seam allowances toward the rectangles.

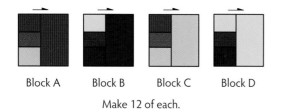

Block A   Block B   Block C   Block D

Make 12 of each.

//Assembling the Quilt

1. Referring to the quilt assembly diagram, right, for block placement, arrange the blocks into eight horizontal rows of six blocks each. Move the blocks around until you're happy with the way fabrics work together, but in order to preserve the basic design, reposition or trade blocks diagonally.

2. Pin and sew the blocks into rows. Press the seam allowances in opposite directions from row to row.

Word to the Wise

I like to mark the top of each block with a piece of chalk to make sure I don't accidentally rotate it while sewing.

3. Pin and sew the rows together in sets of two each, pressing seam allowances to one side. Sew the sets together into two sections, and press the seam allowances to one side. Join the sections and press the seam allowances to one side.

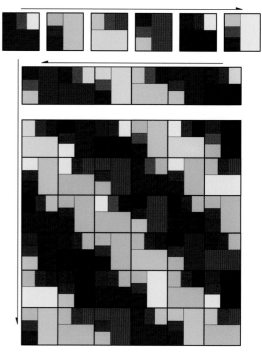

Quilt assembly

//Adding the Borders

1. Sew the charcoal 2" x 42" strips together end to end to make one long strip. Press the seam allowances open.

2. Measure the length of the quilt top through the center and cut two border strips to that measurement. Pin and sew the strips to the sides of the quilt. Press the seam allowances toward the border.

3. Measure the width of the quilt top through the center, including the borders just added, and cut two border strips to that measurement. Pin and sew the strips to the top and bottom of the quilt. Press the seam allowances toward the border.

4. Repeat steps 1–3 using the multicolored 5½" x 42" strips to add the outer border.

//Finishing the Quilt

Layer and baste your quilt top with backing and batting, and then add quilting and binding.

For details on any of these steps, go to ShopMartingale.com/HowtoQuilt for free downloadable information.

LONG SHOT

I love coin quilts and always have a lot of fun making them. (One of my favorite coin quilts was featured on the cover of my book New Cuts for New Quilts, published by Martingale in 2006.) I've always wanted to make a quilt with the coins rotated vertically rather than horizontally, which is what I did for "Long Shot." I also moved the colors around a bit so they don't all line up perfectly. As an alternative, these blocks would look great with the seams going horizontally in a setting of three blocks across and six blocks down. Try it on your design wall to see if you like it; you'd have two blocks left over.

Finished quilt: 56½" x 83½"
Finished block: 11" x 17"

//Materials

Yardage is based on 42"-wide fabric. Fat quarters measure approximately 18" x 22".

3 yards of medium-gray solid for blocks

1 fat quarter *each* of 2 different reds and 2 different dark blues for blocks

1 fat quarter *each* of orange, turquoise, green, brown, and black-and-white prints for blocks

⅝ yard of dark-blue print for outer border

¼ yard of blue print for narrow vertical strips

¼ yard of white-and-black print for inner border

¼ yard of turquoise print for middle border

⅔ yard of fabric for binding

5¼ yards of fabric for backing

65" x 92" piece of batting

Fabric Tips

Choose one main color to repeat through all the blocks. I chose a medium gray. For the "long shots," choose an assortment of colors that look good together. I think the long shots look best when made out of small-scale prints that contrast well with the main color. If you have a stash of fat quarters, this would be a great time to use them up.

//Cutting

From the medium-gray solid, cut:
6 strips, 16" x 42"; crosscut into 11 rectangles, 16" x 20"

From *each* of the 9 fat quarters, cut:
1 rectangle, 16" x 20" (9 total)

From the blue print, cut:
4 strips, 1" x 42"

From the white-and-black print, cut:
3 strips, 1½" x 42"

From the turquoise print, cut:
3 strips, 1½" x 42"

From the dark-blue print, cut:
3 strips, 5½" x 42"

From the binding fabric, cut:
8 strips, 2½" x 42"

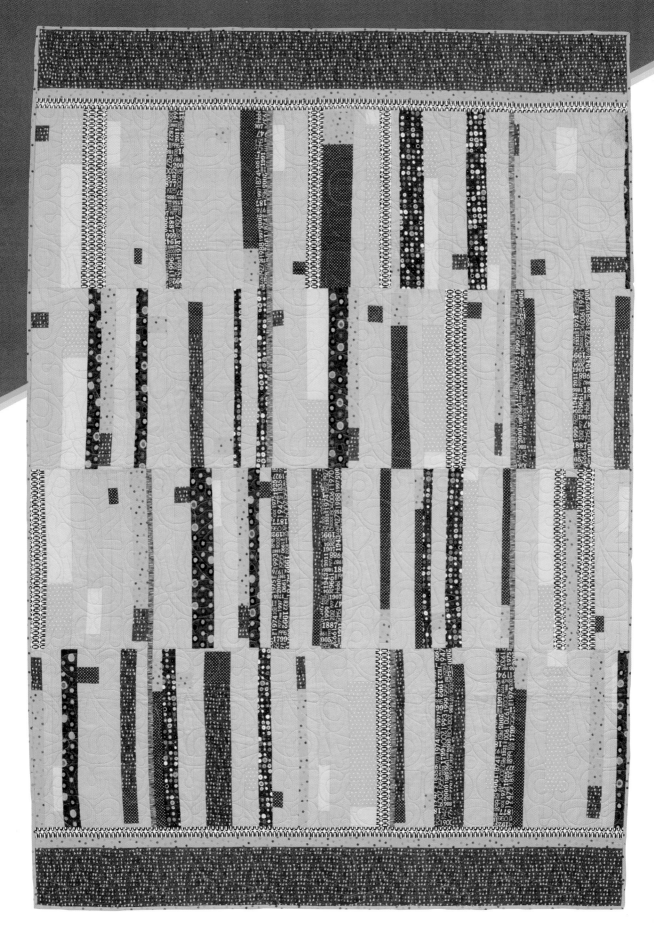

"Long Shot," designed and pieced by Karla Alexander, machine quilted by Loretta Orsborn

//Making the Blocks

1. Arrange six of the 16" x 20" rectangles right side up into a fabric deck, alternating three different colors with three gray rectangles. Arrange one deck of four 16" x 20" rectangles, alternating two different colors with two gray rectangles.

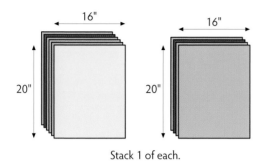

Stack 1 of each.

2. Working with one deck at a time, cut a deck into three stacks. I varied my cuts from 3" to 6" in the lower portion of the deck. The upper section will create the longer strips, or "long shots," in the quilt top. The narrow cuts will create the small squares and rectangles. Shuffle the deck by peeling the top layer from the center stack and placing it at the bottom of that stack. Peel the top two layers from the third stack and place them at the bottom of that stack. Leave the large upper section in place.

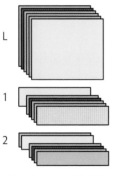

Make 2 cuts and shuffle.

3. Pin and sew each layer together. Rearrange the narrow pieces in each layer as needed so that you don't have two gray strips next to each other. Press the seam allowances to one side.

4. Repeat steps 2 and 3 with the remaining deck to yield four more blocks for a total of 10 blocks.

5. Trim the remaining gray and assorted 16" x 20" rectangles to 16" x 19". Then, referring to the illustration below, arrange the 10 pieced blocks with the rectangles into four decks, alternating pieced blocks and rectangles. Keep the rectangles right side up and rotate the pieced blocks so that the narrow strips alternate position within each deck.

Make 2 decks   Make 2 decks
of 6 layers.   of 4 layers.

6. Work with two decks at a time, beginning with the six-layer decks. Cut each deck in half vertically, or a little off-center, making the widths identical for each deck. Switch one stack from the first deck with the second one; check that they are both the same width. Set one deck aside and work with one deck at a time.

7. Make three vertical cuts through all layers of both sides of the deck.

8. Shuffle the deck by removing the top layer from the first stack and placing it at the bottom of the stack. Then, keeping the pieces in their original stacks, shuffle as many layers as you like to the back, controlling the look of the layers as you go. You may or may not want to have two colors side by side. Experiment with each layer until you like how it looks. You won't be able to see the other five layers underneath, but you can always peek at them or rearrange them as you sew.

9. Piece the blocks together one layer at a time. Remove the top eight pieces and lay them next to your sewing machine. At this point you can rearrange them again if you like, moving the columns into different positions. I usually kept the wider pieces on the outer edges, making it easier to trim the blocks to size after sewing. When you're ready to join the pieces, begin sewing at opposite ends from column to column to prevent warping. Press the seam allowances to one side. Trim the block to 11½" x 17¾".

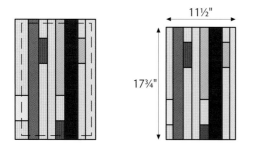

10. Repeat steps 6–9 to complete the second deck of six. Then repeat the steps using the two decks of four layers each.

Assembling the Quilt Top

1. Arrange the blocks into four horizontal rows of five blocks each, moving the blocks around until you are satisfied with the layout.

2. Sew the blocks into sections as shown in the illustration below to prepare for adding the blue print strips. These extra "long shots" are optional and can be eliminated if you like the arrangement better without them.

3. Cut two blue 1" x 42" strips into 35" lengths. Pin and sew one strip to the right edge of section 1. Pin and sew the other strip to the right edge of section 4. Press all seam allowances toward the blue strips.

4. Cut one blue 1" x 42" strip into a 17¾" length. Pin and sew the strip between the blocks of section 6. Press.

5. Piece the remainder of the blue strip from step 4 with the remaining blue 1" x 42" strip, and then trim to a 52½" length. Pin and sew to the right edge of section 2. Press.

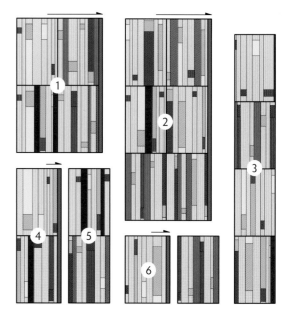

6. Pin and sew the sections together as follows, pressing seam allowances to one side. Sew section 4 to section 5. Then sew this combined section to section 1.

7. Pin and sew section 2 to section 6 and press. Pin and sew this combined section to section 3. Press. Pin and sew the two combined sections together and press.

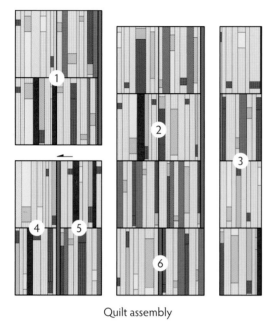

Quilt assembly

// Adding the Borders

1. Sew the white-and-black inner-border strips together to make one long strip. Repeat with the turquoise middle-border strips and the dark-blue outer-border strips.

2. Measure the width of the quilt top through the center and cut two segments of each border strip to that measurement. Make the cuts so that the seam allowances won't be directly on top of each other when you sew them together.

3. Sew the inner, middle, and outer border strips together. Make two border units. Press the seam allowances toward the dark-blue border.

4. Pin and sew the combined border units to the top and bottom of the quilt top. Press the seam allowances toward the border.

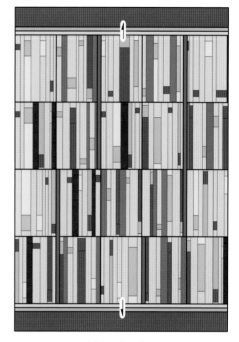

Adding borders

// Finishing the Quilt

Layer and baste your quilt top with backing and batting, and then add quilting and binding.

For details on any of these steps, go to ShopMartingale.com/HowtoQuilt for free downloadable information.

BETWEEN DARK AND DAWN

I'm always drawn to black-with-white and white-with-black fabrics and love the quirky patterns they come in. If you want to liven up a quilt, adding a small amount of black-and-white fabric will often do the trick. With this quilt, I decided to do the opposite by using a higher percentage of black and white. Then I introduced sparks of dark-pink batiks to highlight and frame the prints into what appear to be four patches.

Finished quilt: 57½" x 76½"
Finished block: 9½" x 9½"

// Materials

Yardage is based on 42"-wide fabric.

⅜ yard *each* of 6 different black prints for blocks*

⅜ yard *each* of 6 different white prints for blocks*

⅛ yard *each* of 6 different dark-pink batiks for rims**

⅝ yard of fabric for binding

5 yards of fabric for backing

66" x 85" piece of batting

*You can also use 1½ yards of a single print.

**You can also use ⅝ yard of a single print.

Fabric Tips

I chose an equal mix of black-with-white and white-with-black prints for the main portion of the blocks. (These are referred to as "black prints" and "white prints" in the materials list.) Any print pattern will work, as long as you can sort your choices into definite darks and lights. For the accents, I chose a mix of reds and oranges. You don't need a lot of accent fabric for each block, so stash pieces would be perfect here. I also tried the blocks with bright turquoise accents. I liked the turquoise and contemplated using a mix of different colors in the finished quilt, but in the end I felt that one colorway looked best.

// Cutting

From *each* of the 6 black and 6 white prints, cut:
  1 strip, 10½" x 42"; crosscut into 4 rectangles, 10" x 10½" (48 total)

From *each* of the 6 dark-pink batiks, cut:
  3 strips, 1" x 42"; crosscut into 8 strips, 1" x 10½" (48 total)

From the binding fabric, cut:
  7 strips, 2½" x 42"

"Between Dark and Dawn," designed and pieced by Karla Alexander, machine quilted by Loretta Orsborn

//Making the Blocks

1. Arrange the 10" x 10½" rectangles right side up into eight decks of six layers each. Alternate three black and three white rectangles in each deck, and stack each deck differently from one to the next. Line up the edges as perfectly as you can.

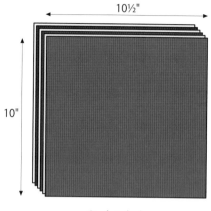

Stack 8 decks.

2. Work with one deck at a time and slice it in half horizontally across the 10½" width, creating two 5" x 10½" sections.

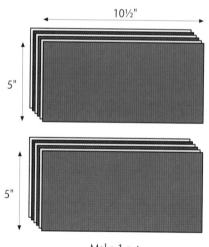

Make 1 cut.

3. Sew a 1" dark-pink strip to the upper edge of each piece in the lower deck section. Press the seam allowances toward the strip and replace it on your cutting mat, underneath the other sections.

4. Slice vertically through both the upper and lower sections, 5½" from the left edge of the decks, to create two sections 5½" wide and two sections 5" wide. Label the sections with letters A–D as shown.

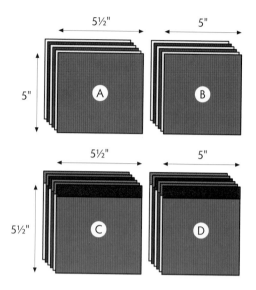

5. Shuffle the top layer of section D to the bottom of the stack. The top layer will have three dark sections and one light. Rotate section C clockwise 90° as shown. Pin and sew section C to section D. Press the seam allowances toward C. Swap the position of sections A and B and sew them together; press the seam allowances toward A. Pin and sew the sections together. Press the seam allowances toward section A/ B.

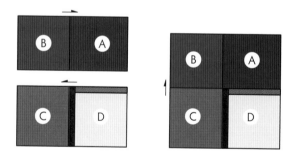

6. Repeat step 5 to complete the remaining five blocks.

7. Repeat steps 2–5 for the remaining decks.

//Assembling the Quilt

1. Arrange the blocks into eight horizontal rows of six blocks each, moving them around until you are happy with the layout. I chose to orient the blocks so that the dark-pink accents created squares. Don't hesitate to try different layouts, as you can create many different patterns simply by changing the rotation of the blocks.

2. Pin and sew four blocks together as shown to create a jumbo block. Be careful to match the seam intersections, and to press seam allowances in opposing directions. Repeat to complete 12 jumbo blocks. When pressing the final block seam, alternate the pressing direction from block to block.

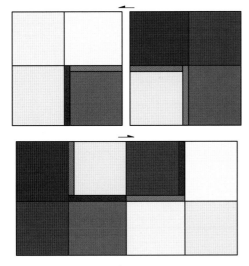

Make 12.

3. Pin and sew the jumbo blocks together in four horizontal rows of three blocks each. Press the seam allowances in opposite directions from row to row.

4. Pin and sew the rows together in two sets of two each. Press the seam allowances to one side. Sew the two sections together, and press the seam allowances to one side.

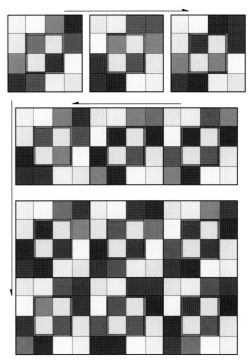

Quilt assembly

//Finishing the Quilt

Layer and baste your quilt top with backing and batting, and then add quilting and binding.

For details on any of these steps, go to ShopMartingale.com/HowtoQuilt for free downloadable information.

HANG UPS

This little quilt is a lot of fun and could really be considered a stash quilt as far as the flags are concerned. I wanted an uneven line of flags in a multitude of different colors hanging against a light background. You can follow the fabric requirements word by word or improvise based on what you have in your stash. Either way, once you get the "hang" of sewing the flags, it's a very simple quilt to make. I can easily imagine it with the colorways changed, featuring light flags against a light-blue or dark background.

Finished quilt: 62½" x 79¾"

//Materials

Yardage is based on 42"-wide fabric.

2⅛ yards of off-white solid for background

¼ yard *each* of 2 orange, 2 turquoise, 2 medium-gray, 2 dark-blue, 2 green, and 2 black-and-white prints for flags*

⅓ yard of red print for horizontal strips

½ yard of dark-blue print for inner border

1⅛ yards of turquoise print for outer border

⅔ yard of fabric for binding

4⅞ yards of fabric for backing

71" x 88" piece of batting

*One fat eighth (9" x 22") of each is enough if the fabric measures at least 21" wide after removing the selvage.

Fabric Tips

Once you decide on your background fabric, you can begin choosing the colors and prints for the flags. If you have good contrast between the two, your flags will show up well. I opted for a light background with a mix of both light and dark prints for my flags. I picked a few grays as well, plus a couple of prints with a small percentage of white in the pattern. I also used two different shades of off-white for the background; however, to simplify matters, the fabric requirements list just one. Fan out your choices against your background and take a step back to help you visualize how they will all look together. As long as you have the correct number of rectangles for both the background and the flags, you can make your quilt in whatever colors you'd like.

//Cutting

From *each* of the 12 prints for flags, cut:
1 rectangle, 7" x 21" (12 total)

From the off-white solid, cut:
8 strips, 7½" x 42"; crosscut into:
    12 rectangles, 7½" x 21"
    8 squares, 7½" x 7½"
2 strips, 1¼" x 42"
3 strips, 2" x 42"
7 strips, 4" x 42"

Continued on page 38

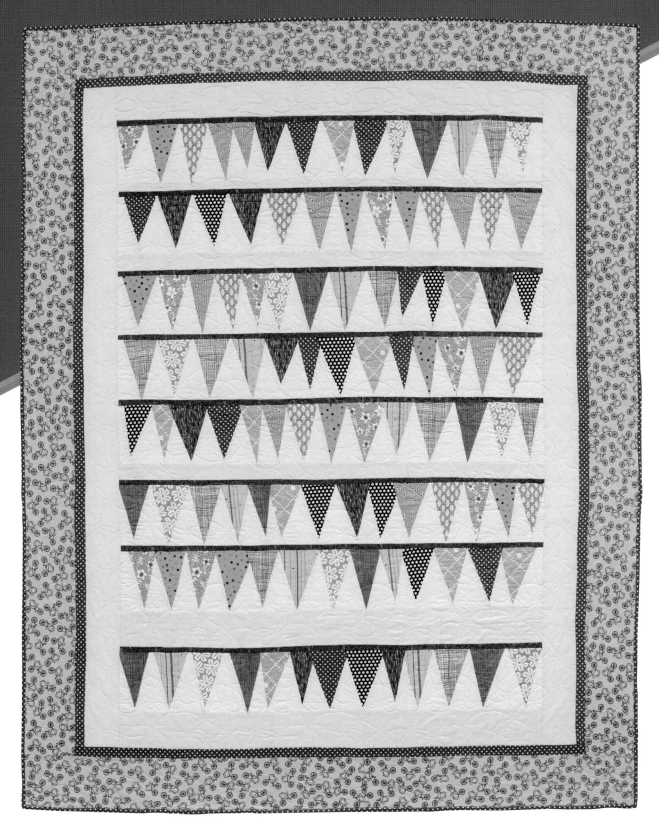

"Hang Ups," designed and pieced by Karla Alexander, machine quilted by Loretta Orsborn

Continued from page 36

From the red print, cut:
  9 strips, 1" x 42"

From the dark-blue print, cut:
  6 strips, 2" x 42"

From the turquoise print, cut:
  7 strips, 5½" x 42"

From the binding fabric, cut:
  8 strips, 2½" x 42"

//Making the Rows

1. Stack four off-white 7½" x 21" rectangles with four different print 7" x 21" rectangles right side up. Begin with the off-white on the bottom and alternate off-white with colored rectangles, ending with a colored rectangle on the top of the deck. Carefully center the colored rectangles on top of the off-white so that ¼" of white show at both the top and bottom of each layer in the deck. Stack a total of three decks.

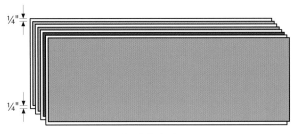

Stack 3 decks.

2. Measure 2" in from each end of the deck and mark eight angled cuts with a chalk pencil as shown. When you're happy with the angles and spacing, make the cuts through all layers.

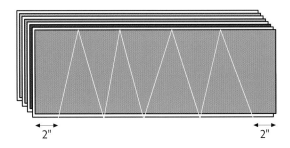

3. Shuffle the deck from left to right. Peel the top layer from the first wide-bottomed triangle and place it at the bottom of that stack. Peel the top two layers from the next stack and place them at the bottom of that stack. Continue shuffling, increasing the number that you move to the

bottom of each stack, until you reach the last stack. Leave the first and last stacks unshuffled. You don't have to follow these shuffling instructions exactly. Just make sure you always have colored triangles in the correct positions. Sometimes I didn't want the same two fabrics on the outer edges, so I shuffled the colors within each stack until I liked what I saw.

Shuffle.

4. Lift the top nine pieces off the deck and place them next to your sewing machine, keeping them in their shuffled order for sewing.

5. Start with the piece on the left edge and pin it to the second piece; offset the edges by about ¼" so that when the pieces are opened up, the bottom horizontal edges line up. Check the alignment and reposition as necessary before sewing the pieces together. Press the seam allowances toward the darker fabric. Add the third piece in the same manner, pinning and offsetting so the *top* edge aligns. The colored triangles are smaller, so they will never match the length of the white pieces. Aligning at the top keeps the points of the flags from being too close to the edge and ensures a nice, sharp, floating point.

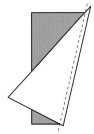

6. Continue pinning and sewing until all pieces have been added. Press the seam allowances to one side. If you have excess fabric where the points line up, you can trim it off.

7. Press your blocks and trim the top and bottom edges so that the unit measures approximately 6¼" to 6½" tall. Be sure to leave at least ¼" below the flag points so that they won't be cut off when you join them to the horizontal strips. Don't

worry about the right and left edges at this time, since they will be trimmed later. Sew the remaining layers of the deck to make eight blocks. Keep the height the same for all of them, but it's OK if the horizontal width varies from one to the next.

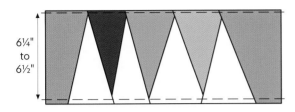

6¼"
to
6½"

8. Repeat steps 2–7 for the two remaining decks. Make a total of 24 blocks.

9. Separate the blocks into two stacks, A and B. The A stack should have 12 blocks with a colored fabric on each end, and the B stack should have 12 blocks with white on each end.

10. Arrange the blocks into eight horizontal rows of three blocks each: four rows with two A blocks and one B block and four rows with two B blocks and one A block.

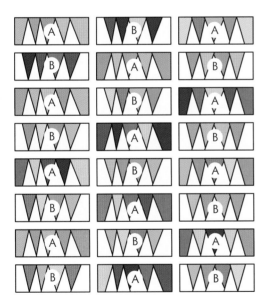

11. To create the flag on the outer edge of each A block, press the edge of the block under at an angle as shown. Place an off-white 7½" square over the fold and mark the angle with a chalk marker. Trim the off-white fabric ¼" from the chalk line. Unfold the pressed triangle and trim it ¼" from the fold. Pin and sew the pieces together, aligning the top edges. Press and trim the off-white

section even with the A block. Repeat this procedure for the eight A blocks that are on the outside edges of the rows.

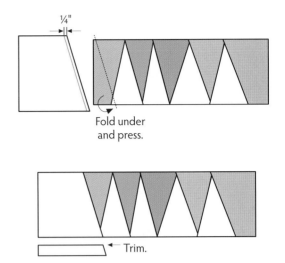

¼"

Fold under and press.

Trim.

12. To join the A and B blocks into rows, fold and press under the end piece of the A blocks as you did before to create the flags in the center of the row. Place the end of the adjacent B block over the fold and mark the angle with a chalk marker. Trim the fabric ¼" from the chalk line. Unfold the block with the pressed angle and trim it ¼" from the fold. Pin the blocks together and open up before sewing to make sure the edges will be aligned when sewing is complete. Sew the blocks together and press the seam allowances to one side. Continue until all the rows are complete.

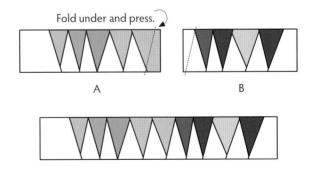

Fold under and press.

A   B

13. Measure the length of all rows and make a note of the shortest one. Trim the other rows to that length.

14. If your rows are longer than 42", you will need to piece the nine red 1" x 42" strips together end to end to make one long length. Cut eight strips to the length used in step 13. Pin and sew a strip to the top edge of each of the rows, along the

wide edges of the colored flags. Press the seam allowances toward the red strip.

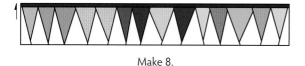

Make 8.

Assembling the Quilt

1. If your measurement from step 13 of "Making the Rows" is longer than 42", sew the off-white 1¼" x 42" strips together into one long length. Repeat with the 2" x 42" strips and the 4" x 42" strips. Using the measurement from step 13, cut one length from the 1¼"-wide strip, two lengths from the 2"-wide strip, and three lengths from the 4"-wide strip.

2. Lay out the eight flag rows horizontally, moving them around until you are happy with the arrangement. Place the off-white 4" strips at the top and bottom of the layout. Referring to the diagram below, use the remaining off-white strips to fill in between the rows as desired, leaving some rows without a background strip.

3. Pin and sew the rows together in six sets of three sections each and one set of two rows without a horizontal strip. Press the seam allowances toward the red strips when possible; press the remaining seam allowances toward the off-white strips.

4. Pin and sew the sections together and press.

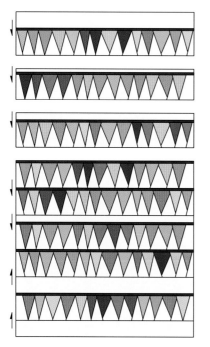

Quilt assembly

5. Measure the length of the quilt top through the center, and cut two pieces to that length from the remaining off-white 4"-wide strip. Pin and sew the pieces to both sides of the quilt top. Press the seam allowances toward the strips just added.

Adding the Borders

1. Sew the dark-blue inner-border strips together end to end to make one long strip. Press the seam allowances open.

2. Measure the length of the quilt top through the center and cut two border strips to that measurement. Pin and sew the strips to the sides of the quilt. Press the seam allowances toward the border.

3. Measure the width of the quilt top through the center, including the borders just added, and cut two border strips to that measurement. Pin and sew the strips to the top and bottom edges of the quilt. Press the seam allowances toward the border.

4. Repeat steps 1–3 to add the turquoise outer border.

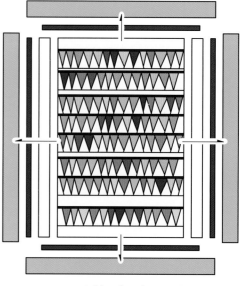

Adding borders

Finishing the Quilt

Layer and baste your quilt top with backing and batting, and then add quilting and binding.

For details on any of these steps, go to ShopMartingale.com/HowtoQuilt for free downloadable information.

SQUARED STRAITS

I wanted to create a soft, quiet-looking quilt, but I also wanted to add some intensity to the overall feel. Light-value gray and brown batiks achieve the soft, mellow effect, while vibrancy is injected by yellows, golds, and greens, as well as the narrow blue strips, or straits, surrounding each block. Three different block sizes keep the design from being too predictable, and uneven sashing adds to the randomness, allowing the blocks to float about the quilt top.

Finished quilt: 56½" x 73"
Finished block: 11½" x 11½"

Materials

Yardage is based on 42"-wide fabric.

1⅛ yards *each* of 2 light-sandy-brown batiks for block borders

⅝ yard *each* of 8 gold, medium-yellow, light-yellow, and yellow-green batiks for blocks

⅔ yard of bright-blue print for block accent rims

¼ yard of dark-blue batik for middle border

1⅔ yards of medium-sandy-brown batik for inner and outer borders

⅝ yard of fabric for binding

4⅝ yards of fabric for backing

65" x 81" piece of batting

Fabric Tips

Choose a mix of golden and light-value yellow and green batiks that blend well, but not to the extent that they look like one fabric. Batiks work nicely as there are so many choices for every imaginable color. The goal is to create a block with colors that blend from one to another without any hard lines. I chose a bright blue to frame the blocks once they were complete. Preview different colors with your blocks and choose one that creates a strong contrast so your blocks will stand out.

Cutting

From *each* of the 8 gold, yellow, and green batiks, cut:
  1 rectangle, 9½" x 24" (8 total)
  1 rectangle, 8½" x 24" (8 total)

From the remaining pieces, cut a *total* of:
  5 rectangles, 5½" x 20"

From the light-sandy-brown batiks, cut a *total* of:
  5 strips, 2½" x 42"; crosscut into 7 strips, 2½" x 10", and
    7 strips, 2½" x 12"
  5 strips, 3½" x 42"; crosscut into 8 strips, 3½" x 9", and 8 strips,
    3½" x 12"
  5 rectangles, 5½" x 7"

Continued on page 43

"Squared Straits," designed and pieced by Karla Alexander, machine quilted by Loretta Orsborn

Continued from page 41

From the bright-blue print, cut:

20 strips, 1" x 42"; crosscut into:

    30 strips, 1" x 9"

    14 strips, 1" x 10"

    16 strips, 1" x 8"

    10 strips, 1" x 6"

    10 strips, 1" x 7"

From the dark-blue batik, cut:

6 strips, 1" x 42"

From the medium-sandy-brown batik, cut:

6 strips, 2" x 42"

7 strips, 6" x 42"

From the binding fabric, cut:

7 strips, 2½" x 42"

//Making the Blocks

1. Arrange the eight yellow, gold, and green 9½" x 24" rectangles right side up into a fabric deck. The order doesn't matter—after the cutting and shuffling is complete, you will have one layer of each color in each stack. Align the edges as perfectly as possible. Use a chalk marker to get an idea of how wide to make seven cuts. Try not to cut the exact same width each time; vary your cuts as you go, making them all at least ¾" apart. Use your ruler and make sure your cuts are straight. You can cut one layer at a time, then restack as you cut if you feel that your cuts would be more accurate.

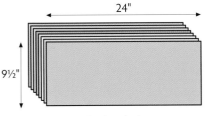

Stack 1 deck.

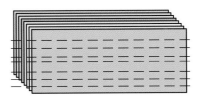

Make 7 cuts.

2. Shuffle the deck by peeling the top layer from the first stack and placing it at the bottom of that stack. Peel the top two layers from the next stack

and place them at the bottom of that stack. Continue in this manner until you reach the last stack, which should be left as it is. After shuffling, you should have eight different fabrics showing on the top layer.

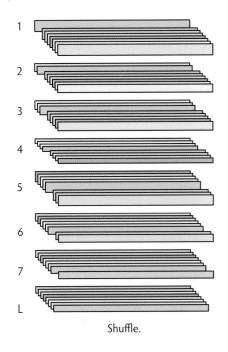

Shuffle.

3. Remove the top eight strips from the deck to sew together. This part is a lot of fun since you can mix the strips up as you sew, arranging the order as you please. Just make sure you only have the eight pieces from the top layer, which, if measured, would have a total width of 9½". I like to rearrange my strips and keep the wider ones on the outer edges, giving me wiggle room when trimming to an even width later.

4. Sew the first two strips together using a scant ¼" seam allowance; offset each by approximately one strip width to create a 45° angle as shown. After you have sewn the first strip, flip the set upside down and begin sewing on the same end where you just finished. This will help keep your strip set straight and prevent it from curving and becoming distorted. Continue adding strips, keeping the outer edge at an approximate 45° angle. Once you have joined all the strips, press the seam allowances to one side, and then continue with the remaining layers.

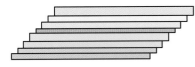

Make 8 strip sets.

5. Trim the strip sets to a 5" width. Use your ruler to trim the right edge of each strip set to a 45° angle as shown. Rotate the strip set 180° so that the cut edge is on your left. Align the 45° line of your ruler with a seam line or raw edge and place the ruler edge at the raw edge of the strip set. Cut a triangle. Rotate the ruler, align the 45° line as before, and cut a second triangle. Continue cutting; each strip set should yield four quarter-square triangles for a total of 32.

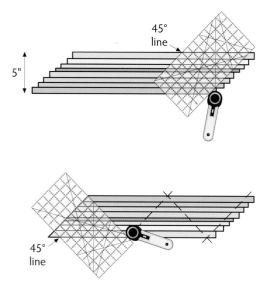

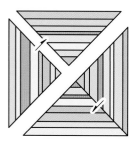

Cut 4 triangles from each strip set.

6. Arrange four triangles into a block as shown. Pin and sew the triangles into pairs. Press the seam allowances in opposite directions. Pin and sew the halves together, and press the seam allowances to one side. Trim the points that extend beyond the edge of the block (sometimes called dog-ears). Make seven blocks (you'll have four quarter-square triangles left over). Trim each block to 9" x 9".

Make 7.

7. Pin and sew bright-blue 1" x 9" strips to opposite sides of each block. Press the seam allowances toward the strips. Pin and sew bright-blue 1" x 10" strips to the top and bottom of each block. Press the seam allowances toward the strips.

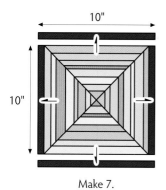

Make 7.

8. Repeat steps 1–5 with the 8½" x 24" rectangles, making seven cuts in each. Trim the width of the sets to 4½". Use your ruler to trim the edge of each set to a 45° angle. Repeat the cutting procedure to cut four quarter-square triangles from each strip set for a total of 32.

9. Repeat step 6 to arrange and sew the triangles into eight blocks. Trim the blocks to 8" x 8".

10. Pin and sew bright-blue 1" x 8" strips to opposite sides of each block. Press the seam allowances toward the strips. Pin and sew bright-blue 1" x 9" strips to the top and bottom of each block. Press the seam allowances toward the strips.

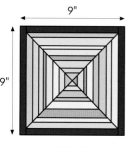

Make 8.

11. Repeat steps 1–5 with the five 5½" x 20" rectangles, making three cuts in each. Sew strips together to make five strip sets. Trim the width of the sets to 3½". Use your ruler to trim the edge of each strip set to a 45° angle. Repeat the cutting procedure to cut four quarter-square triangles from each strip set for a total of 20.

12. Repeat step 6 to arrange and sew the triangles into five blocks. Trim the blocks to 6" x 6".

13. Pin and sew bright-blue 1" x 6" strips to opposite sides of each block. Press the seam allowances toward the strips. Pin and sew bright-blue 1" x 7" strips to the top and bottom of each block. Press the seam allowances toward the strips.

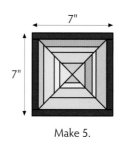

Make 5.

//Adding the Block Borders

1. Add a light-brown 2½" x 10" strip to the top of a large block; press the seam allowances toward the strip. Add a light-brown 2½" x 12" strip to one adjacent side, creating an L shape. You can use the same or a different print on the second side. Press the seam allowances toward the strip. The block should measure 12" x 12". Repeat for the remaining 10" square blocks.

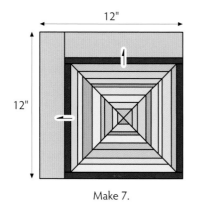

Make 7.

2. Arrange the light-brown 3½" x 9" strips right side up into two decks of four layers each, alternating the two different prints. Slice each deck lengthwise, a little off-center, to create two sections. Peel the top layer from one stack and place it at the

bottom of that stack. Peel the top layer from each of the two stacks and join these pieces to the top and bottom edges of a medium (9" x 9") block. Press the seam allowances toward the strips. Repeat for the remaining medium blocks.

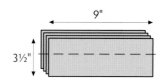

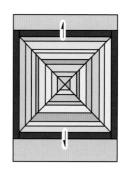

3. Repeat step 2 using the light-brown 3½" x 12" strips. Sew the strips to the sides of the medium blocks. You should have eight blocks that measure 12" x 12".

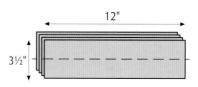

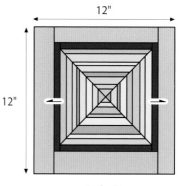

Make 8.

4. Layer the light-brown 5½" x 7" rectangles right side up into a deck, alternating the two different prints as much as possible. Slice the deck across the 5½" width, a little off-center, to create two sections. Peel the top layer from one stack and place it at the bottom of that stack. Peel the top layer from each of the two stacks and join these pieces to the top and bottom edges of a small (7" x 7") block. Press the seam allowances toward the strips. Repeat for the remaining small blocks. You should have five blocks that measure 7" x 12".

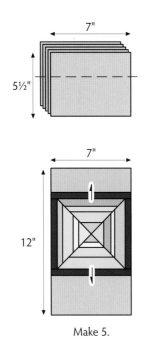

Make 5.

//Assembling the Quilt

1. Arrange the blocks into five horizontal rows of four blocks each as shown in the quilt assembly diagram, right. Each row must include one small block positioned vertically. Move the other blocks around until you are happy with the layout. You can rotate the medium and large blocks in any direction you choose, but the small blocks can only be rotated 180°. I positioned my blocks as follows:
   Row 1: medium, large, small, large
   Row 2: medium, small, medium, large
   Row 3: medium, large, small, medium
   Row 4: medium, small, medium, large
   Row 5: large, large, small, medium

2. Pin and sew the blocks into rows, pressing seam allowances in opposite directions from row to row. Pin and sew the rows together in pairs. Pin and sew the fifth row to a combined row, and then sew

the three sections together, pressing seam allowances to one side.

Quilt assembly

//Adding the Borders

1. Sew the medium-brown 2" x 42" strips together end to end to make one long strip. Press the seam allowances open. Measure the length of the quilt top through the center and cut two border strips to that measurement. Pin and sew the strips to the sides of the quilt. Press the seam allowances toward the border.

2. Measure the width of the quilt top through the center, including the borders just added, and cut two border strips to that measurement. Pin and sew the strips to the top and bottom edges of the quilt. Press the seam allowances toward the border.

3. Repeat steps 1–3 to add the dark-blue middle border and the medium-brown outer border. Press all seam allowances toward the just-added borders.

//Finishing the Quilt

Layer and baste your quilt top with backing and batting, and then add quilting and binding.

For details on any of these steps, go to ShopMartingale.com/HowtoQuilt for free downloadable information.

REFLECTIONS

This quilt was designed using modified Rail Fence blocks. The piecing method keeps the light values in the center of the block, with colors fading to gray on one edge and blue on the other. There are a lot of different possible layouts, and I encourage you to experiment. I'm eager to try this in a red-white-and-blue version for a patriotic look.

Finished quilt: 59½" x 75½"
Finished block: 8" x 8"

//Materials

Yardage is based on 42"-wide fabric.

½ yard *each* of 2 different medium-blue prints for blocks*

½ yard *each* of 2 different medium-turquoise prints for blocks*

½ yard *each* of 2 different light-blue-with-white prints for blocks*

½ yard *each* of 2 different light-white-and-gray prints for blocks*

½ yard *each* of 2 different light-gray-and-white prints for blocks*

½ yard *each* of 2 different medium-gray prints for blocks*

½ yard *each* of 2 different dark-gray prints for blocks*

1⅓ yards of blue print for border

⅝ yard of fabric for binding

5 yards of fabric for backing

68" x 84" piece of batting

You can also use ⅞ yard of a single fabric.

Fabric Tips

For a soft effect, I chose a range of colors from medium blue and light turquoise to white, blending into light and medium gray. Small- and medium-scale prints with nonstylized or subtle designs work best and help tie the prints together from piece to piece. When choosing your mix of fabric, look for prints that are multicolored but that still read as roughly one color.

//Cutting

From the prints for blocks, cut a *total* of:**
49 rectangles, 10" x 13"

From the blue print, cut:
7 strips, 6" x 42"

From the binding fabric, cut:
7 strips, 2½" x 42"

**Cut 3 from each print plus 1 from each of the 7 different color categories. Cut 7 from each if you're using just 7 fabrics.*

"Reflections," designed and pieced by Karla Alexander, machine quilted by Loretta Orsborn

//Making the Blocks

1. Arrange the 10" x 13" rectangles into seven decks of seven layers each, in the following order: medium blue on the bottom, turquoise, light blue, white, light gray, medium gray, and dark gray. The colors should flow from dark to light and back to dark. Arrange each deck in the same color order, but try to use different prints in each one. Don't be concerned if some are identical, however.

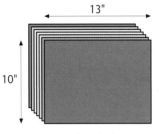

Stack 7 decks.

2. Using a ruler and rotary cutter, make six straight vertical cuts through all seven layers as shown. Make sure the width of each cut is at least 1½". Vary your cuts so they are always different within each deck as well as from deck to deck.

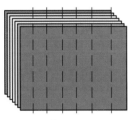

Make 6 cuts.

3. Referring to the illustration, shuffle the deck. Leave the first column on the left as is; peel the top layer from the second column and place it at the bottom of that stack. Peel the top two layers from the third column and place them at the bottom of that stack. Continue shuffling the deck, moving one additional layer to the bottom each time. You should have seven different prints showing on the top layers.

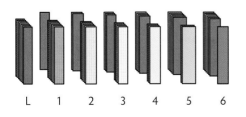

L   1   2   3   4   5   6

4. Peel the seven top strips of different widths from the deck. Place a pin through each of the remaining seven stacks to keep their layers together, or use a paper layout as described on page 7. If you happen to get the layers mixed up, you can get straightened out by adding up the strip widths. The total width of all the strips before being sewn together should always equal 13".

5. Lay the seven strips beside your sewing machine and make sure they are lined up in the same order used when stacking: medium blue, turquoise, light blue, white, light gray, medium gray, and dark gray. Use this color order for each layer and for all the decks. The only thing that will change from layer to layer is the width of the strips. Piece the strips together, beginning at opposite ends each time you add a new strip. This will keep the set nice and straight and prevent distortion. Press the seam allowances to one side.

6. Repeat steps 4 and 5 to make seven blocks. Complete the remaining six decks in the same manner to yield a total of 49 blocks. You will use 48 blocks; one is extra. Press the seam allowances toward the medium blue in 24 of the blocks and toward the dark gray in the other 24.

7. Trim all of the blocks to 9" x 9". Don't be concerned if your blocks aren't as large as mine; just make sure that all the blocks are the same size.

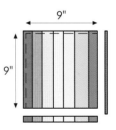

8. Separate the blocks into two stacks of 24 blocks each, based on the direction the seam allowances are pressed. Position each block with the medium-blue strip horizontal along the top edge. Slice one stack in half from corner to corner as shown, creating two half-square triangles from each block. Slice the blocks in the other stack in half from corner to corner in the opposite direction.

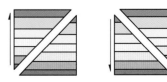

9. Pair a triangle with a long blue edge from the first stack with one from the second stack. Pin and sew the triangles together. Press the seam allowances open to reduce bulk. Repeat with the remaining triangles, pairing the triangles with blue edges together and the triangles with dark-gray edges together. You will have 24 blocks of each, for a total of 48. The blocks should measure approximately 8½" square. It doesn't matter if they are larger or smaller than 8½"; just make sure they are all the same size.

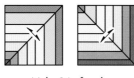

Make 24 of each.

//Assembling the Quilt

1. Referring to the quilt assembly diagram for block placement, arrange the blocks into eight horizontal rows of six blocks each. Position the blocks with dark-gray edges in the center of the quilt top and place the blocks with blue edges on the outer edges.

2. Pin and sew the blocks into rows, pressing seam allowances in opposite directions from row to row.

3. Pin and sew the rows together in sets of two each, pressing seam allowances to one side. Sew the sets together into two sections, and press the seam allowances to one side. Join the sections and press the seam allowances to one side.

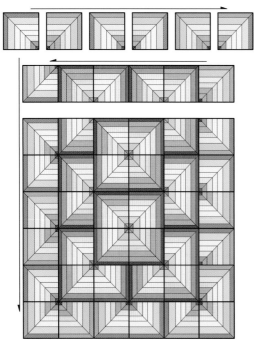

Quilt assembly

//Adding the Border

1. Sew the blue 6"-wide strips together end to end to make one long strip.

2. Measure the length of the quilt top through the center and cut two border strips to that measurement. Pin and sew the strips to the sides of the quilt. Press the seam allowances toward the border.

3. Measure the width of the quilt top through the center, including the borders just added, and cut two border strips to that measurement. Pin and sew the strips to the top and bottom of the quilt; press the seam allowances toward the border.

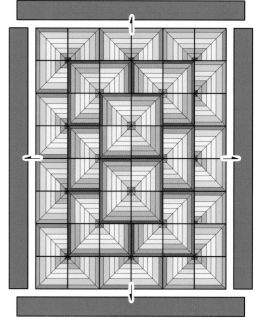

Adding borders

//Finishing the Quilt

Layer and baste your quilt top with backing and batting, and then add quilting and binding.

For details on any of these steps, go to ShopMartingale.com/HowtoQuilt for free downloadable information.

RENDEZVOUS

This quilt is a lot of fun to make and goes together fairly effortlessly. Each block is different from one to the next. The use of two different colorways for the sashing accentuates the dark and yellow block backgrounds. To finish off the color selection, I sprinkled in hints of blue for sparkle. This quilt provides a good opportunity to raid your stash if you happen to have one. Enjoy!

Finished quilt: 70½" x 89½"
Finished block: 17" x 17"

//Materials

Yardage is based on 42"-wide fabric.

½ yard *each* of 4 different lemon-yellow prints for blocks

½ yard *each* of 4 different black or dark-gray prints for blocks

⅝ yard of black print for block borders

⅝ yard of orange print for block borders

¼ yard *each* of 2 different white-and-black prints for blocks

⅜ yard of blue print #1 for blocks and cornerstones

¼ yard of blue print #2 for blocks

1⅓ yards of white-and-black print for sashing

1½ yards of dark-gray print for border

¾ yard of fabric for binding

5½ yards of fabric for backing

79" x 98" piece of batting

Fabric Tips

Choose a mix of black-and-white and white-and-black prints to mix with lemon yellow as the main colors. Hints of orange and blue here and there will add interesting contrast to the varying sizes of squares and rectangles. Choose colors that contrast well with the main colors.

//Cutting

From *each* of the 4 lemon-yellow prints, cut:
  1 strip, 4¼" x 42"; crosscut into 4 rectangles, 4¼" x 10"
    (16 total)
  2 strips, 4¼" x 42"; crosscut into 6 rectangles, 4¼" x 8"
    (24 total)

From *each* of the 4 black or dark-gray prints for blocks, cut:
  3 strips, 4¼" x 42"; crosscut into:
    4 rectangles, 4¼" x 10" (16 total)
    6 rectangles, 4¼" x 8" (24 total)

From blue print #1, cut:
  1 strip, 4¼" x 42"; crosscut into 4 rectangles, 4¼" x 10"
  2 strips, 2½" x 42"; crosscut into 20 squares, 2½" x 2½"

From blue print #2, cut:
  1 strip, 4¼" x 42"; crosscut into 4 rectangles, 4¼" x 10"

Continued on page 53

"Rendezvous," designed and pieced by Karla Alexander, machine quilted by Loretta Orsborn

Continued from page 51

From *each* of the 2 white-and-black prints for blocks, cut:

I strip, 4¼" x 42"; crosscut into 4 rectangles, 4¼" x 10" (8 total)

From the black print for block borders, cut:

12 strips, 1½" x 42"; crosscut into 12 strips, 1½" x 15½", and 12 strips, 1½" x 17½"

From the orange print, cut:

12 strips, 1½" x 42"; crosscut into 12 strips, 1½" x 15½", and 12 strips, 1½" x 17½"

From the white-and-black print for sashing, cut:

16 strips, 2½" x 42"; crosscut into 31 strips, 2½" x 17½"

From the dark-gray print for border, cut:

8 strips, 6" x 42"

From the binding fabric, cut:

9 strips, 2½" x 42"

//Making the Blocks

1. Arrange the 4¼" x 10" rectangles right side up into eight decks of six fabrics each: yellow, black or dark gray, white-and-black, black or dark gray, yellow, and blue. Line up the edges as perfectly as possible. Stack each deck differently from one to the next. The order of layers won't matter too much, as you will have the opportunity to rearrange the colors when shuffling after the deck has been cut.

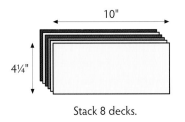

Stack 8 decks.

2. Working with one deck at a time, measure 4¾" from the left edge and cut through all six layers. Slide the right half of the stack to the right and place a pin through all layers to keep it together. Slice the left half vertically and then horizontally

to make a four-patch block. You can center your cuts exactly or cut a little off-center. I cut a variety of both.

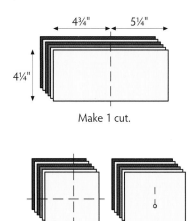

Make 1 cut.

Make 2 cuts.

3. Shuffle the four-patch portion of the deck by peeling the top layer from the upper-left stack and placing it at the bottom of that stack. Peel the top two layers from the upper-right stack and place them at the bottom of that stack; peel the top three layers from the lower-right stack and place them at the bottom of that stack. Leave the fourth stack as it is. You can shuffle each stack as many times as you want, as long as you keep each piece in the same stack and don't have any of the same prints side by side.

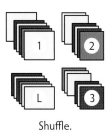

Shuffle.

4. Peel the top layer from each of the four-patch stacks. Sew the top two pieces together, and then sew the bottom two pieces together. Press the seam allowances in opposite directions. Sew the two rows together. For variety, you can flip one row 180° so the four-patch seams don't line up. Press the seam allowances to one side. Continue sewing each layer to complete all six four-patch blocks. Set the blocks aside. Don't worry about keeping them in the original shuffled order.

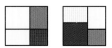

5. Slice the remainder of the deck vertically into two stacks, keeping them at least 1" wide. Peel the top three layers off the left stack and place them at the bottom of that stack. Peel four layers from the right stack and place them at the bottom of that stack.

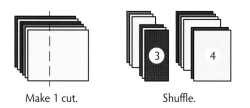

Make 1 cut. Shuffle.

6. Lay out the six four-patch blocks so that the shorter sides are horizontal and the longer sides are vertical. Add a layer from both the left and right stacks from step 5. The overall pattern will look best with the four-patch block positioned between the two pieces, but you can switch some of them if desired. Arrange the blocks so that three have at least one yellow edge and three have at least one black or dark-gray edge. You can swap the step 5 pieces from block to block as long as each block has one piece from the left shuffled stack and one piece from the right. Sew the pieces and four-patch blocks together. Press the seam allowances away from the four-patch. Make a total of six units.

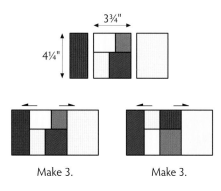

Make 3. Make 3.

7. Repeat steps 2–6 using the remaining decks.

8. Separate the block units into one stack of 24 with yellow edges and one stack of 24 with black or dark-gray edges. If you have one with both colors, it can go in either stack.

9. Sew a yellow 4¼" x 8" rectangle to one long side of each yellow-edged unit. Press the seam allowances toward the large rectangle. Sew a black or dark-gray 4¼" x 8" rectangle to one side of each black- or gray-edged unit. Press the seam allowances toward the large rectangle.

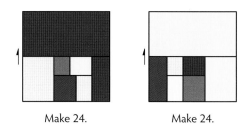

Make 24. Make 24.

10. Arrange the units into groups of four, each with edges of the same color and with the large rectangles facing outward. Sew the top two units together and then sew the bottom two units together. Press the seam allowances in opposite directions. Pin and sew the pieced sections together and press. Repeat to complete a total of six blocks with yellow edges and six blocks with black or dark-gray edges.

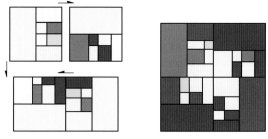

Make 6 of each.

11. Sew black-print 1½" x 15½" strips to the sides of each block with yellow edges. Press the seam allowances toward the strips. Sew black-print 1½" x 17½" strips to the top and bottom. Press the seam allowances toward the strips. Repeat to add the orange print strips to the six blocks with black or dark-gray edges.

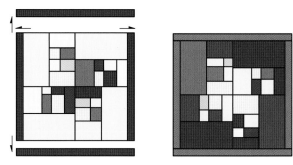

Make 6 of each.

Assembling the Quilt

1. Sew three white-and-black 2½" x 17½" strips together with four 2½" squares of blue print #1 to make a sashing row. Press the seam allowances toward the strips. Make five rows.

Make 5.

2. Arrange the blocks in four horizontal rows of three blocks each, alternating the two colorways. Add four white-and-black 2½" x 17½" sashing strips to each row as shown in the quilt layout. Place sashing rows between each of the block rows and at the top and bottom of the layout.

3. Sew each of the rows together with the four 17½"-long sashing strips. Press the seam allowances toward the sashing. Replace the rows back in the original layout.

4. Pin and sew the two center rows with the sashing row in the center. Press the seam allowances toward the sashing.

5. Pin and sew the upper section to the middle section, and then add the lower section. Press the seam allowances toward the sashing.

Adding the Border

1. Sew the dark-gray 6" x 42" strips together end to end to make one long strip.

2. Measure the length of the quilt top through the center and cut two border strips to that measurement. Pin and sew the strips to the sides of the quilt. Press the seam allowances toward the border.

3. Measure the width of the quilt top through the center, including the borders just added, and cut two border strips to that measurement. Pin and sew the strips to the top and bottom of the quilt; press the seam allowances toward the border.

Finishing the Quilt

Layer and baste your quilt top with backing and batting, and then add quilting and binding.

For details on any of these steps, go to ShopMartingale.com/HowtoQuilt for free downloadable information.

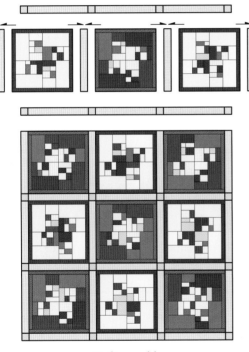

Quilt assembly

SHATTERED

The inspiration for this quilt came to me when I visited our city's annual summer art fair. I saw several displays of mosaic work in the form of wall art, garden art, and mirror and picture frames. The images stuck in my mind and soon I began subconsciously building a quilt that I thought resembled mosaics. One morning I got up and began working on my creation, and by the end of the day, "Shattered" was almost done. This was my first attempt at a mosaic-themed quilt, and I have to say, this project simply took on a life of its own. It was fun to make and I can't wait to try it again—maybe in a smaller-scale version using dark gray and medium brown. I think a mellow-toned miniature would be awesome!

Finished quilt: 63½" x 84½"
Finished block: 21" x 21"

//Materials

Yardage is based on 42"-wide fabric. Fat quarters measure approximately 18" x 22".

1⅛ yards *each* of 4 dark-purple and dark-blue batiks for blocks

1 fat quarter *each* of 6 assorted crimson-red batiks for block centers

⅔ yard *each* of 4 assorted turquoise batiks for block borders

⅔ yard of fabric for binding

5¼ yards of fabric for backing

72" x 93" piece of batting

Fabric Tips

I picked batiks for the rich, clear colors they offer. When it comes to the colorway, the choice is completely up to you. Begin by choosing a focal color for the center blocks and then a second color for the fractured path that surrounds them. Subtle batiks, tone-on-tone prints, or other prints that appear as a solid from a distance work best for this quilt. Next you will need a dark contrasting print to separate all the pieces. I chose crimson reds for the center blocks, bright turquoise for the path, and deep, dark blues and purples for the fracture lines. You could also consider a medium gray for those lines to resemble grout in tile work.

//Cutting

From *each* of the 6 crimson-red fat quarters, cut:
2 squares, 10" x 10" (12 total)

From *each* of the 4 turquoise batiks, cut:
1 strip, 16" x 42"; crosscut into 10 rectangles, 4" x 16" (40 total)
1 strip, 4" x 42"; crosscut into 2 rectangles, 4" x 16" (8 total)

From *each* of the 4 purple and blue batiks, cut:
1 strip, 16" x 42"; crosscut into 10 rectangles, 4" x 16" (40 total)
1 strip, 4" x 42"; crosscut into 2 rectangles, 4" x 16" (8 total)
15 strips, 1" x 42" (60 total); crosscut a *total* of 192 strips, 1" x 9"

From the binding fabric, cut:
8 strips, 2½" x 42"

"Shattered," designed and pieced by Karla Alexander, machine quilted by Loretta Orsborn

//Making the Block Centers

1. Arrange the red 10" squares right side up into two decks of six fabrics each. Line up the edges as perfectly as possible.

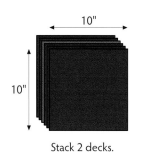

Stack 2 decks.

2. Use a chalk marker to draw five fracture lines on each deck, similar to those shown. You don't have to follow the diagram exactly; draw your own lines and simply brush the chalk away if you want to make changes. I tried to make my cuts look like a fractured piece of glass. Working with one deck at a time, cut on the chalk lines through all layers. The numbers indicate the cutting order.

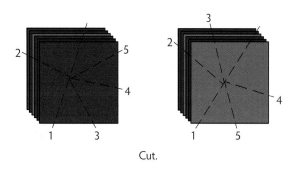

Cut.

3. Shuffle the deck by peeling the top layer from the first stack and placing it at the bottom of that stack. Peel the top two layers from the next stack and place them at the bottom of that stack. Continue until all but one stack has been shuffled; leave that one in place. You should have a mix of six different reds showing on the top layer and in each layer underneath.

Shuffle.

4. Tape a few pieces of paper together and use straight pins to fasten the shuffled stacks to the paper to keep the layers in order. Draw the outline of each stack onto the paper. Add numbers to your paper to indicate sewing order, and place a safety pin in the top layer of stack 1 so you will always be able to identify it as the top layer. Remove the straight pins from the stacks numbered 1 and 2 and place the stacks next to your sewing machine.

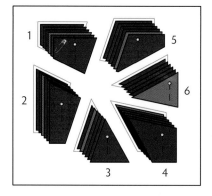

5. Lay a dark-purple or blue 1" x 9" strip along the edge of stack 1 that is next to stack 2, and trim six strips to that length plus an extra inch for wiggle room. I mixed up the purple and blue strips so that each block is scrappy and random. Chain piece the strips to one side of all the pieces from stack 1, without breaking the thread between strips. Once you reach the end of the last strip, clip the thread from the sewing machine and pull the set toward you until you reach the pin, identifying the first layer.

6. Add a piece from stack 2 to the opposite edge of the 1" strip. Pin it in place first and open it up to make sure the outer edges of the block line up. If they don't, readjust where you begin sewing. Chain piece the six pieces from stack 2.

7. Remove the chained pieces from the sewing machine. Before moving to the ironing board, pull the sets toward you and clip the thread one block at a time. Place the first unit on your work surface or on your lap, right side up. Place the next set right on top of the first one. Continue to clip and stack the units until you reach the unit with the pin. Flip the stack upside down and take it to your ironing board. Press the unit that is on top of the stack first, pressing the seam allowances toward the narrow strip from the wrong side. Flip the piece right side up and press one more time. Place the pressed unit aside, right side up. Repeat to press the next unit, and then place it right side up on top of the first pressed unit. Continue pressing each unit. When you press the last one, it should have the pin in the corner to let you know it is the top layer. Lay a purple or blue 1" x 9" strip next to the long side of a unit from step 7. Trim six pieces as before and then chain piece the strips to the units. Press the seam allowances toward the strips. Return the stack of combined units to the paper layout.

8. Working with the other section of the block, add strips in the order shown, chain piecing as before.

9. Sew the two sections of the block together. Press the seam allowances toward the center strip. Trim and square up the block centers to 9½" x 9½".

10. Repeat steps 2–10 to sew blocks from the remaining deck. Make a total of 12 block centers.

Making the Block Borders

1. Stack the purple and blue 4" x 16" rectangles right side up into 12 decks of four fabrics each. Align the edges as neatly as possible.

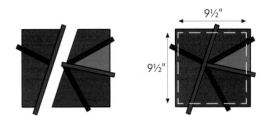

Stack 12 decks.

2. Working with one deck at a time, make an off-center vertical cut through the 16" length of the deck, cutting through all four layers. Once you complete your first deck, experiment with the remaining decks, placing your cut in a different place each time. The cut can also be slightly angled if you like. Make sure that the strips are all at least 1¼" wide. Peel the top layer off the left stack and place it at the bottom of that stack. Slide the right half of the cut deck about 10" to the right.

Make 1 cut.

3. Stack the turquoise 4" x 16" rectangles right side up into 12 decks of four fabrics each. Align the edges as neatly as possible.

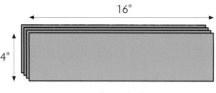

Stack 12 decks.

4. Place one turquoise deck between the two halves of the deck cut in step 2. With right sides together, chain piece the four purple or blue strips to the left edge of the turquoise strips. When you finish adding the last piece, clip the thread and pull the set toward you. Open the strips as you sew and add the remaining purple or blue strips to the right edge of the turquoise strips. Clip the sets apart and press the seam allowances toward the turquoise fabric. Put a pin through the strip sets to keep them together as a group and set aside. Repeat steps 2–4 and complete the remaining decks for a total of 48 strips.

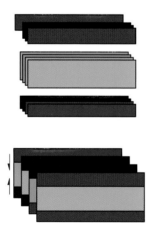

5. Choose one strip set from each of the twelve groups and layer them right side up into three decks of four. Repeat two more times for a total of twelve decks. Rotate the strips 180° from layer to layer as shown, above right, to offset the different widths. Use a chalk marker and draw four fracture lines similar to the diagram. You don't have to follow the diagram exactly; draw your own lines and simply brush the chalk away if you want to make changes. Just make sure your lines are angled and not stright up and down. The sharper the

angle, the better. Work with one deck at a time and cut on the chalk lines through all layers.

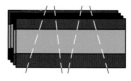

6. Leave the first stack on the left as it is. Starting with the second stack, shuffle the deck by peeling the top layer from the stack and placing it at the bottom. Peel the top two layers from the next stack and place them at the bottom of that stack. Repeat with the fourth stack, peeling and shuffling three layers to the bottom. Leave the last stack on the right as it is.

7. Keep a stack of purple and blue 1" x 9" strips next to your sewing machine as you sew. You will need a total of 16 strips for each deck. Place a safety pin in the upper-left corner of the first layer on the first stack to help identify the top layer. Chain piece a strip to the left edge of all four segments from stack 1, with the narrow strip extending about ½" above the top edge of the segment. Add the strips to all four layers, and then clip the thread from the sewing machine and pull the combined sets toward you until you reach the set with the safety pin. Open the sets as you sew and add the segments from the second stack, right sides together, to the right edge of the strip. Continue sewing in this manner until all the segments have been added. Clip the sets apart and press the seam allowances toward the narrow strips. Trim the block borders to 6½" x 15½".

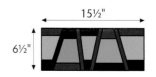

15½"

6½"

8. Repeat steps 5–7 for the remaining decks. Make 48 block borders.

//Assembling the Blocks

1. Choose four block borders and one red block center. Arrange the borders around the center block to create the "path."

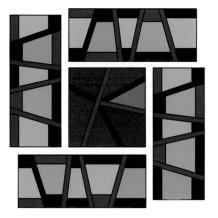

2. Sew a block border to the block center with a partial seam, leaving approximately 3" unsewn. Finger-press the seam allowance toward the red center. Working counterclockwise, sew the second strip to the entire length of the block center and the first border. Finger-press the seam allowances toward the block center. Repeat to add the third and fourth borders. Return to the first border and complete the seam. Press the seam allowances toward the block center.

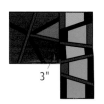

3"

Sew.

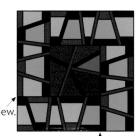

Sew.

Complete the seam.

3. Repeat steps 1 and 2 to make a total of 12 blocks. You can make the blocks as you go, or complete all the decks first so you will have more variety to choose from when adding the borders to the block centers. Making the blocks from one deck at a time gives you an opportunity to determine if you need wider or narrower cuts on your decks.

//Assembling the Quilt

1. Arrange the blocks in four horizontal rows of three blocks each. Move the blocks around until you are satisfied with the layout.

2. Pin and sew the blocks in each row together. Press the seam allowances in opposite directions from row to row.

3. Pin and sew the rows together in two sets of two, and then sew the two sections together. Press the seam allowances to one side.

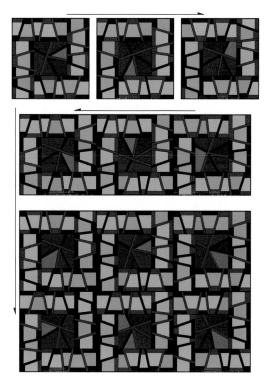

Quilt assembly

//Finishing the Quilt

Layer and baste your quilt top with backing and batting, and then add quilting and binding.

For details on any of these steps, go to ShopMartingale.com/HowtoQuilt for free downloadable information.

WINDMILL WAY

The way the colors blur from light to dark around the dark center squares in this quilt remind me of spinning blades on a windmill. Each fabric color appears in a different width in each of the blocks. The accent border is made using an improvisational technique I use when I want to add just a little more punch to a project. This quilt makes a perfect throw to cuddle up in on a chilly day.

Finished quilt: 54" x 67"
Finished block: 13" x 13"

//Materials

Yardage is based on 42"-wide fabric.

⅝ yard *each* of 6 assorted white, white-and-green, and green prints ranging in value from light to dark

⅛ yard of dark-gray print for block centers

⅜ yard of pink print for first border

¼ yard of gray dot for third (accent) border

1⅛ yards of green print for second and fourth borders

⅝ yard of fabric for binding

3¾ yards of fabric for backing

62" x 75" piece of batting

Fabric Tips

Decide on a colorway, and then choose six fabrics that represent a gradation from light to dark. I wanted a bright, airy look, so I chose a white small-scale print as the lightest fabric, followed by a medium-scale print that has a lightly scattered design on a white background. The third print is denser with less white, and the white eventually disappears completely as the fabrics continue to deepen and evolve to a medium-dark green.

//Cutting

From *each* of the 6 prints for blocks, cut:
  1 strip, 10½" x 42"; crosscut into 2 rectangles, 10½" x 18" (12 total)
  1 strip, 7½" x 42"; crosscut into 2 rectangles, 7½" x 18" (12 total)

From the dark-gray print, cut:
  1 strip, 3" x 42"; crosscut into 12 squares, 3" x 3"

From the pink print, cut:
  5 strips, 2" x 42"

From the gray dot, cut:
  6 strips, 1" x 42"

From the green print, cut:
  6 strips, 6" x 42"

From the binding fabric, cut:
  7 strips, 2½" x 42"

"Windmill Way," designed and pieced by Karla Alexander, machine quilted by Loretta Orsborn

//Making the Blocks

1. Stack the 10½" x 18" rectangles into two decks of six fabrics each. Layer the decks in order of value, with the lightest print on the bottom and the darkest print on top. Stack the 7½" x 18" rectangles into two decks of six fabrics each, again layering from lightest on the bottom to darkest on top.

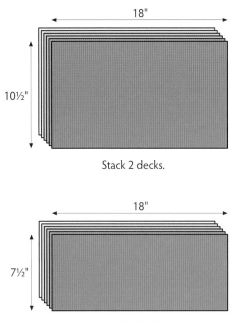

Stack 2 decks.

Stack 2 decks.

2. Cut and sew one deck at a time. To keep my blocks organized, I labeled the 10½" decks as A and the 7½" decks as B. For accuracy, I like to plan the widths of my cuts beforehand. Then I cut one stack at a time, restacking the cut pieces back into the deck. For the 10½" decks, I used the following widths: 1½", 2", 1¾", 1¼", 2", and 2". For the 7½" decks, I used the following widths: 1½", 1½", 1", 1¼", 1¼", and 1". Your cuts don't have to match those widths exactly. Just be sure to make five cuts total, at least ¾" apart, which will shrink down to ¼" after sewing.

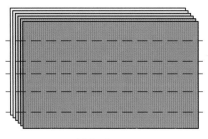

Make 5 cuts.

3. Shuffle the deck as shown. Leave the top stack as is. Peel the top strip from the next stack and place it at the bottom of that stack. Peel the top two strips from the next stack and place them at the bottom of that stack. Continue until you have a gradation of values from the darkest fabric to the lightest. Peel the top layer from each stack. You will have a total of six different-sized strips. If something gets mixed up, keep in mind that the total width of all the strips before being sewn together should always equal 10½" for the A decks and 7½" for the B decks. Place a pin through each of the remaining seven stacks to keep their layers together.

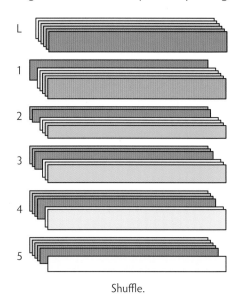

Shuffle.

4. Lay the six strips next to your sewing machine. It doesn't matter if you mix them up—just make sure to always sew them together beginning with the lightest strip, adding the colors in order until you get to the darkest strip, which should always be on the outer edge. Use this order for all the decks. The only thing that will change from layer to layer is the width of the strips. Piece the strips together, beginning and ending at opposite ends each time you add a new strip. This will keep the sets nice and straight and prevent distortion. Press the seam allowances to one side.

5. Repeat steps 2–4 to yield 12 A strip sets and 12 B strip sets. Trim the short edges of the strip sets so that they are even, if necessary. Then trim the long

edges of the A strip sets so that they are 7" wide. Trim the B strip sets so that they are 4½" wide.

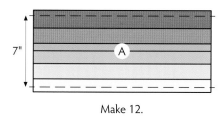

Make 12.

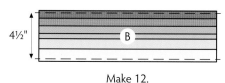

Make 12.

6. Crosscut each A strip set into two sections, 7" x 9½" and 7" x 7". Stack in two different piles. Crosscut each B strip set into two sections, 4½" x 9½" and 4½" x 7", and stack in two different piles.

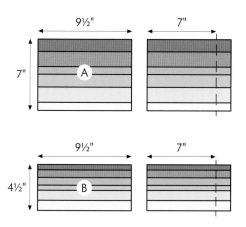

7. Join a pieced 7" square to a dark-gray 3" square with a partial seam, beginning at the edge and sewing for approximately 1". The darkest green should always be closest to the center square. Finger-press the seam allowances toward the square. Open the unit and sew a 7" x 9½" pieced rectangle to the side with the square. Finger-press the seam allowances toward the center square. Working in a clockwise direction, open the set up

and repeat the process to add the 4½" x 9½" and 4½" x 7" pieced rectangles. Then complete the partial seam. Press the seam allowances toward the center block. Make a total of 12 blocks.

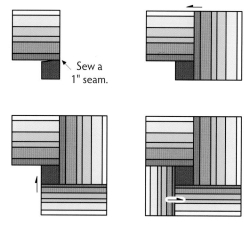

Make 12.

Make a Sample Block

You may want to make a sample block to determine how wide or narrow you like the cuts. To do this, cut a scrap of fabric to the same size as one of the decks. Make the cuts, and then sew the pieces back together using a scant ¼" seam allowance.

//Assembling the Quilt

1. Arrange the blocks in four horizontal rows of three blocks each. Refer to the quilt assembly diagram on page 66, or rotate the blocks as you please.

2. Pin and sew the blocks together into rows. Press the seam allowances in opposite directions from row to row.

3. Pin and sew the rows together in two sets of two, and then sew the two sections together. Press the seam allowances to one side.

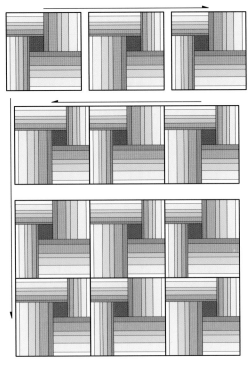

Quilt assembly

//Adding the Borders

1. Sew the pink 2"-wide border strips together end to end to make one long strip.

2. Measure the length of the quilt top through the center and cut two border strips to that measurement. Pin and sew the strips to the sides of the quilt. Press the seam allowances toward the border.

3. Measure the width of the quilt top through the center, including the borders just added, and cut two border strips to that measurement. Pin and sew the strips to the top and bottom of the quilt; press the seam allowances toward the border.

4. Repeat steps 1–3 to add the green 6"-wide outer border strips.

5. To insert the accent border, cut away the top and bottom green borders, 2" from the seam line of the pink border. You can move the accent border closer

to the pink border or farther away if you wish, but cut no closer than 1" from the pink border.

6. Sew the gray-dot 1"-wide strips together end to end to make one long strip. Measure the length of the trimmed-away border strips from step 5 and cut two accent strips to that measurement. Pin and sew each accent strip to a border strip along the long edges. Press the seam allowances toward the accent strips.

7. Pin and sew the new border segments to the top and bottom of the quilt. Press the seam allowances toward the accent strip.

8. Repeat steps 5–7 for the side borders, making sure that the horizontal accent strips line up when you sew the borders back onto the quilt.

Add accent strips.

//Finishing the Quilt

Layer and baste your quilt top with backing and batting, and then add quilting and binding.

For details on any of these steps, go to ShopMartingale.com/HowtoQuilt for free downloadable information.

PAINT CHIPS

Often when I go to a home-improvement store I find myself picking out paint chips ... even when I have no plans to paint anything. I simply love all the colors and usually end up taking 20 or 30 chips home to add to my collection, rearranging them into different assortments and ambitiously dreaming up a project down the road. Recently I began taking pictures of my paint chips in varying arrangements, thinking, "Wow, that would be a cool quilt!" Here's the result. Have fun!

Finished quilt: 52½" x 73"
Finished block: 7½" x 9½"

//Materials

Yardage is based on 42"-wide fabric. Fat quarters measure approximately 18" x 22".

1 fat quarter *each* of 10 different solids: white, off-white, light yellow, gold, lime green, aqua, medium blue, dark blue, dark red, and gray

2⅛ yards of light-gray solid for sashing, inner border, and outer border

⅓ yard of dark-gray solid for middle border

⅝ yard of fabric for binding

3½ yards of fabric for backing

61" x 81" piece of batting

Fabric Tips

Even if you don't have a secret (or not-so-secret) stash of paint chips for inspiration, picking fabrics for this quilt is a breeze. Simply choose a variety of solids in contrasting colors. Feel free to use the colors in the featured quilt as inspiration, or draw from your own favorite palette.

//Cutting

See the cutting guide for fat quarters below.

From the 10 fat quarters, cut a *total* of:
20 rectangles, 11" x 12½"
14 squares, 5" x 5"
4 strips, 1" x 10"
2 rectangles, 1½" x 4"

Continued on page 69

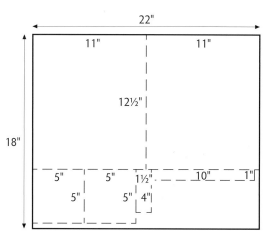

Fat quarter cutting guide.

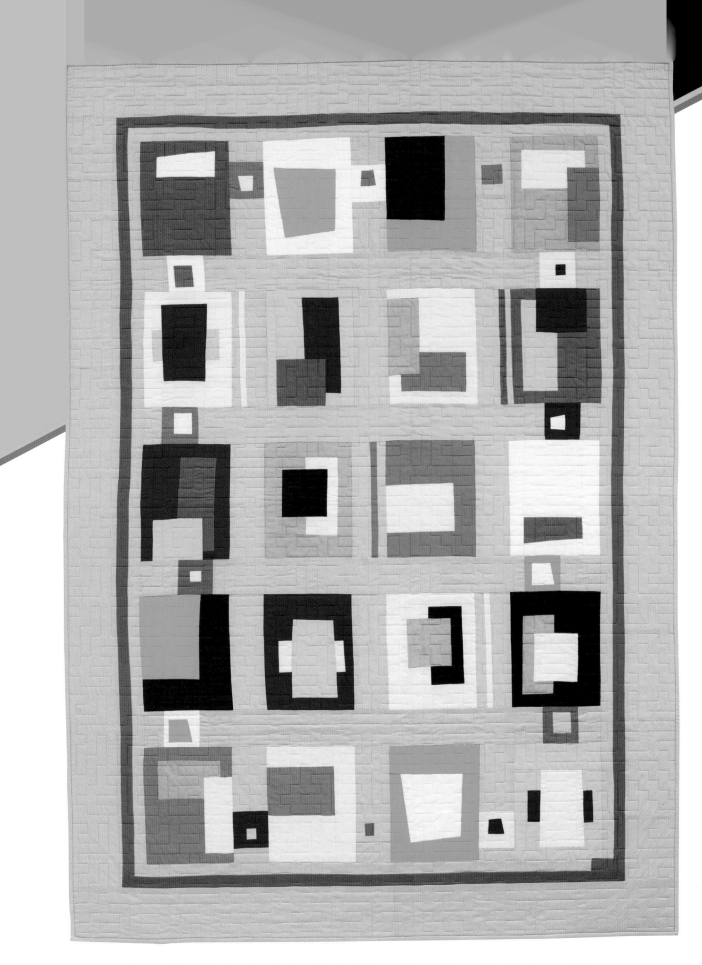

"Paint Chips," designed and pieced by Karla Alexander, machine quilted by Loretta Orsborn

Continued from page 67

From the light-gray solid, cut:
5 strips, 1½" x 42"
8 strips, 3½" x 42"; crosscut 4 of the strips into 15
strips, 3½" x 10"
6 strips, 5" x 42"

From the dark-gray solid, cut:
6 strips, 1½" x 42"

From the binding fabric, cut:
7 strips, 2½" x 42"

//Making the Blocks

When making the Paint Chips blocks, press the seam allowances toward the darker fabrics whenever possible. The instructions are written to make three each of blocks 1–4 and two each of blocks 5–8. Feel free to make a different number of each block if you prefer. In some of the blocks, it's necessary to sew the units first, then combine the units together.

1. Stack the 11" x 12 1/2" rectangles into four decks of three different colors each and four decks of two different colors each. Make sure all layers within a deck contrast from one to the next.

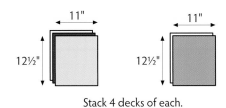

Stack 4 decks of each.

2. Choose one deck of three different colors for each of blocks 1–4. Working with one deck at a time, cut, shuffle, and sew as shown to make three of each block.

Block 1

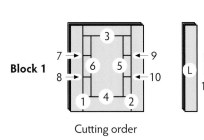

Cutting order

Shuffling order

Sewing order

Block 2

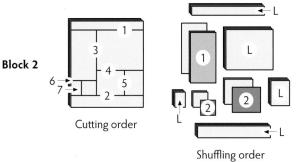

Cutting order

Shuffling order

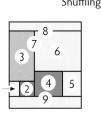

Sewing order

Block 3

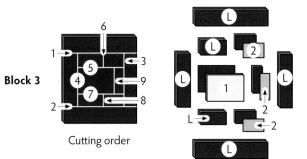

Cutting order

Shuffling order

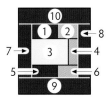

Sewing order

Block 4

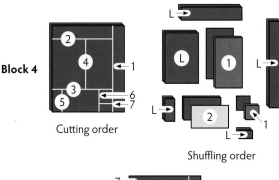

Cutting order

Shuffling order

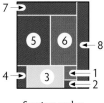

Sewing order

3. Using the decks with two fabrics each, use one deck for each of blocks 5–8. Working with one deck at a time, cut, shuffle and sew as shown to make two of each block.

Block 5

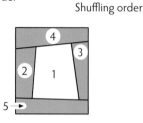

Cutting order

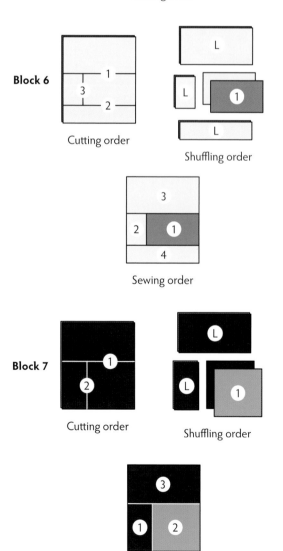

Shuffling order

Sewing order

Block 6

Cutting order

Shuffling order

Sewing order

Block 7

Cutting order

Shuffling order

Sewing order

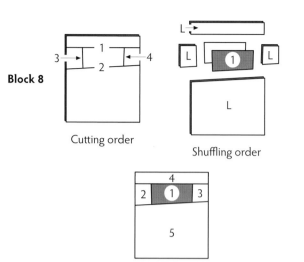

Block 8

Cutting order

Shuffling order

Sewing order

4. Trim all blocks to 8" x 10".

5. Stack the 5" squares into seven decks of two layers each, alternating the colors to create good contrast. Working with one deck at a time, cut and shuffle the decks as shown , varying your cuts for each deck. Sew the blocks, referring to the sewing order. Make a total of 14 blocks and trim each one to 3½" x 3½".

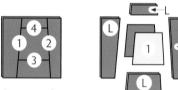

Cutting order

Shuffling order

Sewing order

Sashing blocks

//Assembling the Quilt

1. Lay out the blocks in five horizontal rows of four blocks each, referring to the quilt assembly diagram on page 71. You can move your blocks wherever you like, but keep them oriented vertically. Leave about 4" between all the blocks for the sashing.

2. Add the light-gray 3½" x 10" strips vertically between the blocks and the light-gray 3½" x 42" strips between the rows.

3. Once you are satisfied with the arrangement, lay six of the 3½" sashing blocks on top of the vertical sashing in the top and bottom rows as shown. Slice the sashing where you would like to place a 3½" block. Sew the block between the two pieces of the sliced strip, trim the strip to 10", and replace it in the layout. Repeat for all six sashing blocks.

4. Add the four 1" x 10" strips to the vertical sashing strips where desired. Cut through the sashing strip, sew the narrow strip between the two pieces, press, and replace it in the layout.

5. Pin and sew the blocks and sashing pieces together into horizontal rows. Press the seam allowances toward the sashing strips. Replace the rows in the layout.

6. Remove the selvage edges of the 3½" x 42" sashing strips. Measure the width of the rows and cut each sashing strip to that measurement. Replace the strips in the layout and then position the remaining 3½" sashing blocks on top of the horizontal sashing strips where you would like them. Slice the sashing apart and insert the blocks as you did with the vertical strips. Trim the completed strips to the measured length and replace them in the layout.

7. Sew pieced sashing strips to the bottom of rows 1 through 4. Press the seam allowances toward the sashing. Pin and sew rows 1 and 2 together, and then rows 3 and 4, pressing seam allowances toward the sashing. Add row 5 to the bottom edge of combined rows 3-4. Sew the two sections together, and press the seam allowances toward the sashing.

Adding the Borders

1. Sew the light-gray 1½"-wide border strips together end to end to make one long strip.

2. Measure the length of the quilt top through the center and cut two border strips to that measurement. Pin and sew the strips to the sides of the quilt. Press the seam allowances toward the border.

3. Measure the width of the quilt top through the center, including the borders just added, and cut two border strips to that measurement. Add a solid 1½" x 4" rectangle to one end of each strip. Trim the strip to the measured length again, including as much of the rectangle as you like. Pin and sew the borders to the top and bottom of the quilt; press the seam allowances toward the border.

4. Repeat steps 1–3, omitting the extra rectangles, to add the dark-gray middle border and the light-gray outer border.

Finishing the Quilt

Layer and baste your quilt top with backing and batting, and then add quilting and binding.

For details on any of these steps, go to ShopMartingale.com/HowtoQuilt for free downloadable information.

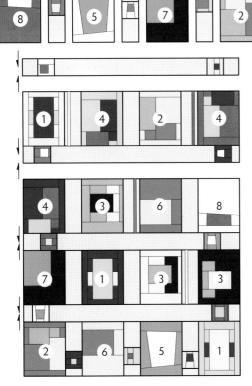

Quilt assembly

LOOSELY WOVEN

I am intrigued by all things woven—baskets, carpet, fabric, chair seats—and I frequently take pictures of these things. I then enlarge the photos to study the way the fibers weave over and under, creating intriguing color changes and different designs. There is always a space between the warp and the weft, no matter how tight or loose the weave. I like to draft quilt designs with both a loose weave and a tight weave, varying the size of the background space. When it comes to piecing a tight weave design, it takes a lot of partial seams to attain the look I want. For this book, I designed something simpler, "Loosely Woven." Happy weaving!

Finished quilt: 55½" x 69½"
Finished block: 7" x 7"

//Materials

Yardage is based on 42"-wide fabric. Fat quarters measure approximately 18" x 22".

⅝ yard of blue-purple print for blocks

⅝ yard of medium-dark blue print for blocks

⅝ yard of medium-purple print with light accents for blocks

⅝ yard of medium-blue-green print for blocks

⅝ yard of medium-green print with yellow accents for blocks

1 fat quarter *each* of 2 different medium-yellow prints with green accents for blocks

1 fat quarter *each* of 2 different medium-light-yellow prints for blocks

1 fat quarter of light-yellow print for blocks

1⅝ yards of blue-purple print for setting squares and border*

⅝ yard of fabric for binding

3¾ yards of fabric for backing

64" x 78" piece of batting

You can use the same blue-purple print that you used for blocks, if you wish.

Fabric Tips

Multicolored or two-color batiks will help the colors blend nicely from light to dark. Ideally, each piece will have either a dark or light accent of the color it will be next to. This helps one colorway lead gracefully into the next. Preview your choices from a distance and make sure they move smoothly from light to dark. The fabric requirements for this quilt will yield extra blocks, so if you have a stash of batiks, this is a great chance to use them. You don't have to use the same exact fabric for each color placement; you can improvise and use a different one for each deck as long as the color and value are the same. The explanation of colors may seem daunting, but once you start looking at your choices, the addition of accent colors will begin to make perfect sense.

"Loosely Woven," designed and pieced by Karla Alexander, machine quilted by Loretta Orsborn

//Cutting

From *each* of the 5 print ⅝-yard pieces, cut:

I strip, 8" x 42"; crosscut into 3 rectangles,
8" x 10½" (15 total)

I strip, 10½" x 42"; crosscut into 4 rectangles,
8" x 10½" (20 total)

From *each* of the 5 yellow fat quarters, cut:

3 rectangles, 8" x 10½" (15 total)

From the blue-purple print, cut:

4 strips, 7½" x 42"; crosscut into 20 squares,
7½" x 7½"

6 strips, 3½" x 42"

From the binding fabric, cut:

7 strips, 2½" x 42"

//Making the Blocks

1. Stack the purple, blue, and green 8" x 10½"
   rectangles into seven decks of five fabrics each.
   Layer the decks in order of value, starting with the
   darkest print on the bottom and the lightest on
   the top. Stack the yellow 8" x 10½" rectangles
   into three decks of five fabrics each. Layer the deck
   in order of darkest print to lightest and then back
   to dark again. Line up the edges as perfectly as
   possible.

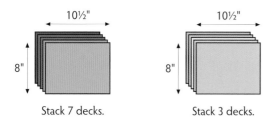

Stack 7 decks.   Stack 3 decks.

2. Beginning with the purple/blue/green fabrics, cut
   and sew one deck at a time. Make four cuts across
   the 8" width of the deck as shown. Vary the width
   of the cuts, keeping them at least 1½" apart. Try
   not to cut the exact same widths for each deck;
   the charm of this method is the random strip
   widths.

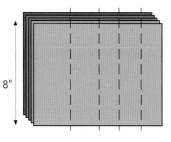

Make 4 cuts.

3. Shuffle the deck, leaving the left stack as it is and
   moving layers to the bottom as indicated. You will
   have a gradation of colors from dark to light. Peel
   off the top layer with a total of five different strips.
   The total width of all the strips before being sewn
   together should always equal 10½". (This is helpful if your strips get mixed up.)

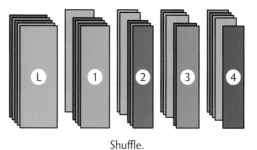

Shuffle.

4. Lay the five strips next to your sewing machine. It
   doesn't matter if you mix them up; just make sure
   to always sew them beginning with the lightest
   strip, adding the colors in order until you get to the
   darkest strip, which should always be on the outer
   edge. Use this same order for all the purple/blue/
   green decks. The only thing that will change from
   layer to layer is the width of the strips. Piece the
   strips together, beginning and ending at opposite
   ends each time you add a new strip. This will keep
   the sets nice and straight and prevent distortion.
   Press the seam allowances to one side.

5. Repeat steps 2–4 to complete the remaining
   purple/blue/green decks, for a total of 35 blocks.
   Trim all blocks to 7½" x 7½". You'll have four
   extra blocks, giving you more options when
   arranging the layout.

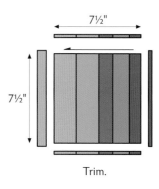

Trim.

6. Repeat steps 2–5 using the yellow decks. When
   arranging the strips in each layer, keep the lightest
   color in the middle and the darkest on the outer
   edges. Make a total of 15 yellow blocks. Three will
   be extra.

//Assembling the Quilt

1. Referring to the quilt layout, arrange the pieced blocks and dark 7½" squares in nine horizontal rows. Place three purple/blue/green blocks and four 7½" squares in the odd-numbered rows. Place four purple/blue/green blocks and three yellow blocks in the even-numbered rows.

2. Pin and sew the blocks together into rows. Press the seam allowances toward the setting squares in the odd-numbered rows. Press the seam allowances toward the yellow blocks in the even-numbered rows.

3. Pin and sew together rows 1 and 2, rows 3 and 4, rows 5 and 6, and rows 7 and 8. Pin and sew combined rows 1-2 to combined rows 3-4. Pin and sew combined rows 5-6 to combined rows 7-8. Pin and sew row 9 to the combined section with rows 5 through 8. Pin and sew the sections together. Press the seam allowances to one side.

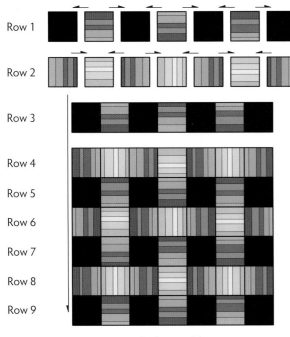

Quilt assembly

//Adding the Border

1. Sew the dark 3½"-wide border strips together end to end to make one long strip.

2. Measure the length of the quilt top through the center and cut two border strips to that measurement. Pin and sew the strips to the sides of the quilt. Press the seam allowances toward the border.

3. Measure the width of the quilt top through the center, including the borders just added, and cut two border strips to that measurement. Pin and sew the strips to the top and bottom of the quilt; press the seam allowances toward the border.

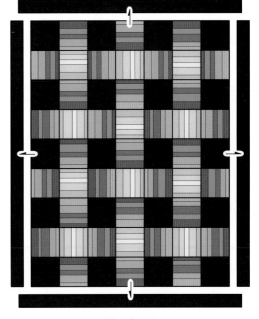

Adding borders

//Finishing the Quilt

Layer and baste your quilt top with backing and batting, and then add quilting and binding.

For details on any of these steps, go to ShopMartingale.com/HowtoQuilt for free downloadable information.

DOT DASH CLICK

I was trying to figure out what to do with a Layer Cake of fabric that I kept moving from one spot to another in my studio. It had been an impulse purchase and I didn't want to cut it up into traditional blocks. However, I knew that if I cut it all in one direction it would shrink up into a rectangle, rather than a square. I decided to go with that option and design around the rectangle. I really liked the results and re-created it using larger 11½" squares from my stash. The idea isn't to have a perfect mix of strips in each block; with this project, you can duplicate or mix it up however you wish. In the end, my quilt reminded me of Morse code characters. I imagine it translated into any message I want for whatever mood I happen to be in!

Finished quilt: 60" x 77"
Finished block: 8½" x 8½"

// Materials

Yardage is based on 42"-wide fabric.

¾ yard *each* of 5 white prints (with accents of chartreuse, gray, black, and aqua) for blocks

¾ yard *each* of 2 black prints for blocks

¾ yard of dark-aqua print for blocks

¾ yard of medium-aqua print for blocks

¾ yard of chartreuse solid for blocks

1⅝ yards of off-white solid for blocks

½ yard of dark-gray solid for blocks

⅔ yard of fabric for binding

4⅞ yards of fabric for backing

68" x 85" piece of batting

Fabric Tips

Choose an assortment of solids mixed with prints, in equal amounts of light and dark, for a look that's trendy and fresh. Include some white-background prints so the strips will float into the white strip on the end of each block. Stripes and polka-dot prints work great. You will need a total of 63 squares, 11½" x 11½", so if you have a stash, consider using some of it in these blocks. Even if your stash yields only one appealing candidate, you can use it as long as it fits with your other choices.

// Cutting

From *each* of the ¾-yard pieces, cut:
2 strips, 11½" x 42"; crosscut into 6 squares, 11½" x 11½" (30 total)

From *each* of the 5 white prints, cut:
2 strips, 11½" x 42"; crosscut into 6 squares, 11½" x 11½" (30 total)

From the dark-gray solid, cut:
1 strip, 11½" x 42"; crosscut into 2 squares, 11½" x 11½"

From the off-white solid, cut:
1 square, 11½" x 11½"
16 strips, 2½" x 42"; crosscut into 63 strips, 2½" x 9"

From the binding fabric, cut:
8 strips, 2½" x 42"

"Dot Dash Click," designed and pieced by Karla Alexander, machine quilted by Loretta Orsborn

//Making the Blocks

1. Stack the 11½" squares into nine decks of seven layers each. Alternate the light fabrics with the dark solid and the dark prints, stacking each deck differently. Line up the edges as perfectly as possible.

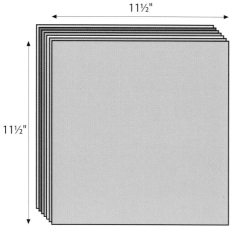

11½"

11½"

Stack 9 decks.

2. Cut and sew one deck at a time. Make six cuts vertically through the deck. Vary your cuts from deck to deck, keeping the cuts at least 1" apart. Try not to cut the same widths for all strips, as the charm of this method lies in the random strip widths.

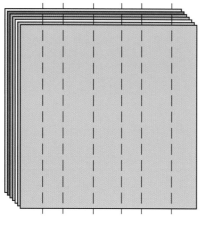

Make 6 cuts.

3. Shuffle the deck as shown, leaving the left stack as is and moving the top layer from the next stack to the bottom of the stack. If you want duplicate fabrics or you'd like to have darks or lights next to each other, shuffle the deck until you are satisfied. Just make sure that each set of strips stays in its

proper stack. Keep in mind that each layer will be a different combination of fabrics.

Shuffle.

4. Chain sew all of the stack 1 pieces to the stack 2 pieces, without breaking the thread between the pieces. When you finish the last set, clip the thread from the sewing machine and pull the combined strips toward you until you reach the first set. Open the pieces up and add the third strip to all seven sets. Continue chain piecing until all of the strips have been added.

5. Remove the units from the sewing machine and clip the strip sets apart. Don't worry about keeping them in order. Press the seam allowances to one side and trim blocks to 8".

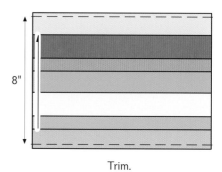

8"

Trim.

6. Cut each block as shown into one segment 7" wide and one segment 1½" wide. Set the narrow segments aside for now.

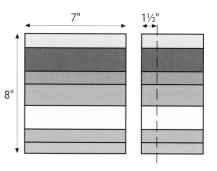

7"   1½"

8"

7. Repeat steps 2–6 with the remaining decks.

8. Match up each of the 7" segments with a 1½" segment. Trim the 1½" segment to 7" long and sew it to a 7" side of the larger segment. Make 63 units. Press the seam allowances toward the 7" × 8" segment.

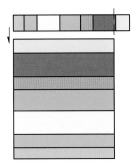

9. Add an off-white 2½" × 9" strip to one side of each unit to complete the blocks. Press the seam allowances toward the white strips.

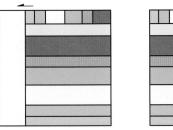 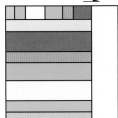

//Assembling the Quilt

1. Refer to the quilt assembly diagram, right, for block placement. Arrange the blocks in nine horizontal rows of seven blocks, alternating the blocks with vertical and horizontal seams. Reposition the blocks as desired until you are satisfied with the arrangement. The blocks could also be positioned with the seams all going in the same direction, or with a variety of vertical and horizontal placements.

2. Pin and sew the blocks into rows. Press the seam allowances in opposite direction from row to row.

3. Pin and sew the rows together in sets of two each, and then into two sections of four. Pin and sew the two sections together, and then add the last row. Press the seam allowances to one side.

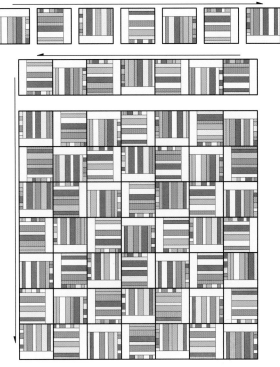

Quilt assembly

//Finishing the Quilt

Layer and baste your quilt top with backing and batting, and then add quilting and binding.

For details on any of these steps, go to ShopMartingale.com/HowtoQuilt for free downloadable information.

ABOUT THE AUTHOR

Karla Alexander lives in Salem, Oregon, in a two-story 1950s house where her studio is just outside the breezeway. The household includes her husband, Don, and the studio dog, Lucy.

Karla loves running, working with concrete, collecting button jars from estate sales, and a few other interesting hobbies, but her main focus always returns to quiltmaking, designing, and teaching.

This is Karla's eighth book on the art of quiltmaking. She also has a pattern line under the name Saginaw Street Quilts and she is a designer for Creative Grids Rulers. As the years have rolled by, she has watched, enjoyed, and been intrigued by the changes in the quilt industry and has always found her niche there, one way or another. Her work can't be pigeonholed into a specific style, as she prefers to work off the cuff and sew what she envisions in her imagination. She doesn't need a predetermined outcome to start a project. With that in mind, she continues designing quilts that always begin with squares or rectangles rather than strips of fabric. She is fascinated and inspired by the patterns found in everyday life—baskets, freeways, the view from an airplane window, door-frames, you name it. The patterns she sees are often reinvented as quilts or provide the springboard for many of her designs.

As a teacher, Karla enjoys immersing herself among her students, knowing there is a lot to be learned from each one of them as well.